Learner Interactions in Massive Private Online Courses

By employing learning analytics methodology and big data in Learning Management Systems (LMSs), this volume conducts data-driven research to identify and compare learner interaction patterns in Massive Private Online Courses (MPOCs).

The uncertainties about the temporal and sequential patterns of online interaction, and the lack of specific knowledge and methods to investigate details of LMSs' dynamic interaction traces have affected the improvement of online learning effectiveness. While most research focuses on Massive Open Online Courses (MOOCs), little is investigating the learners' interaction behaviors in MPOCs. This book attempts to fill in the gaps by including research in the past decades, big data in education presenting micro-level interaction traces, analytics-based learner interaction in massive private open courses, and a case study.

Aiming to bring greater efficiency and deeper engagement to individual learners, instructors, and administrators, the title provides a reference to those who need to evaluate their learning and teaching strategies in online learning. It will be particularly useful to students and researchers in the field of Education.

Di Sun is an associate professor of educational evaluation at Dalian University of Technology. She received her MS and Ph.D. degrees majoring in Educational Evaluation from Syracuse University. Her research interests include Learning Analytics, Educational Data Mining, and Educational Evaluation.

Gang Cheng is an associate professor at The Open University of China, where he directs the Department of Learning Resource and Digital Library. His research interests include Resource and Environment of Digital Learning, Learner Support, and Learning Analytics.

Learner Interactions in Massive Private Online Courses

Di Sun and Gang Cheng

LONDON AND NEW YORK

First published 2023
by Routledge
4 Park Square, Milton Park, Abingdon, Oxon OX14 4RN

and by Routledge
605 Third Avenue, New York, NY 10158

Routledge is an imprint of the Taylor & Francis Group, an informa business

© 2023 Di Sun and Gang Cheng

The right of Di Sun and Gang Cheng to be identified as authors of this work has been asserted in accordance with sections 77 and 78 of the Copyright, Designs and Patents Act 1988. All rights reserved. No part of this book may be reprinted or reproduced or utilised in any form or by any electronic, mechanical, or other means, now known or hereafter invented, including photocopying and recording, or in any information storage or retrieval system, without permission in writing from the publishers.

Trademark notice: Product or corporate names may be trademarks or registered trademarks, and are used only for identification and explanation without intent to infringe.

British Library Cataloguing-in-Publication Data
A catalogue record for this book is available from the British Library

Library of Congress Cataloging-in-Publication Data
A catalog record has been requested for this book

ISBN: 978-1-032-36097-3 (hbk)
ISBN: 978-1-032-36099-7 (pbk)
ISBN: 978-1-003-33021-9 (ebk)

DOI: 10.4324/b23163

Typeset in Times New Roman
by MPS Limited, Dehradun

Contents

List of figures	vii
List of tables	viii
Acknowledgements	ix

    Introduction   1

1 Online Learning Needs Learning Analytics   5
*The Importance of Learner Interaction in Online Learning 5
The Limitations of Traditional Interaction Research in
   Online Learning 5
The Utility of Attaching Importance to LMS Log Data 6
The Need for Applying Academically Sound Methods to
   Investigate Interaction Patterns 7
The Paucity of Learner Interaction Research in MPOCs 8
Definition of Key Terms 10*

2 Traditional Learner Interaction Research in Online Learning   14
*Online Learner Interaction Theory 14
Traditional Research on Online Interaction 16
Discussion 18*

3 LMS Log Data Presenting Interaction Traces   24
*Two Types of Interaction Data Recorded by LMSs 24
Temporal and Sequential Characteristics of Interaction
   Events 26*

4 Interaction Research with Learning Analytics   31
*Learning Analytics methodology 31
Interaction Research with Data from Discourse, Video,
   and Brainwave 33*

Interaction Research with Log Data 35
Interaction Research with Log Data in Particular Topics 39
Discussion 40

5 **Massive Private Open Courses** 52
MOOCs vs MPOCs 52
Comparative Research of Interaction Patterns,
the Lack of MPOCs 53
Summary 55

6 **Research Design of a MPOCs Case** 59
Background and Research Questions 59
Participants and Data Collection 60
Data Pre-processing and Analysis 61
HMMs Measures 63

7 **Results and Discussion Based on the Case** 67
Interpretations of HMMs Results 67
Answers for the Research Questions 78
Discussions Based on Four Research Questions 83

8 **Reflection and Consideration** 87
Implications for MPOCs 87
Reflections of the Paradigm Shift of the Research Method 88
Limitations and Future Plans 91

Index 94

Figures

7.1 HMM of High-achievement group in Learning weeks — 69
7.2 HMM of Low-achievement group in Learning weeks — 72
7.3 HMM of High-achievement group in Exam weeks — 75
7.4 HMM of Low-achievement group in Exam weeks — 77

Tables

6.1	Four datasets	62
7.1	BIC measures of High-achievement group in Learning weeks	68
7.2	HMMs initial probability vector (π) of High-Learning	68
7.3	HMMs transition probability matrix (A) of High-Learning	68
7.4	HMMs output probability matrix (B) of High-Learning	68
7.5	BIC measures of Low-achievement group in Learning weeks	70
7.6	HMMs initial probability vector (π) of Low-Learning	71
7.7	HMMs transition probability matrix (A) of Low-Learning	71
7.8	HMMs output probability matrix (B) of Low-Learning	71
7.9	BIC measures of High-achievement group in Exam weeks	73
7.10	HMMs initial probability vector (π) of High-Exam	73
7.11	HMMs transition probability matrix (A) of High-Exam	74
7.12	HMMs output probability matrix (B) of High-Exam	74
7.13	BIC measures of Low-achievement group in Exam weeks	76
7.14	HMMs initial probability vector (π) of Low-Exam	76
7.15	HMMs transition probability matrix (A) of Low-Exam	77
7.16	HMMs output probability matrix (B) of Low-Exam	77
7.17	Distribution of major activities of two groups in Learning weeks	78
7.18	Distribution of major activities of two groups in Exam weeks	80
7.19	Distribution of major activities of High-achievement group in two course-processes	81
7.20	Distribution of major activities of Low-achievement group in two course-processes	82

Acknowledgements

With the greatest respect and affection, for my dearest advisor.
Prof. Li Chen

Introduction

Distance education is the education of students who may not always be physically present at a school (Kaplan & Haenlein, 2016). The arrival of the Internet in the late 1980s marked distance education evolving into a new era: online learning. As the newest development in distance education, online learning has grown very fast over the past decades. By the fall of 2013, nearly 30% of all postsecondary students were enrolled in some kind of online courses (Snyder, de Brey, & Dillow, 2016).

Based on LMSs and Internet technology, online learning allows learners to engage in learning from anywhere and usually anytime (Labaree, 2004). It is a way of lifelong learning and provides opportunities for individuals to build valuable life and professional skills (Inoue, 2007). With consistent increase in enrollment of online learning, all learners, whether inside or outside the walls of the college, gain the right to learn without the barriers of time and space (Allen & Seaman, 2016). According to advocates, online learning is an educational practice based on the belief that all learners should have the opportunity to learn, and therefore they must be given the necessary support to learn (Wilson, 2004).

Advocates believe that with advanced technology, a wide range of teaching and learning methods can be carried out in online learning to simulate face-to-face instructions; and therefore, learners online are able to learn the same content and to get at least the same learning achievements as learners in face-to-face instructions (Allen, Bourhis, Burrell, & Mabry, 2002; Bernard et al., 2004; Browning, 1999; Cavanaugh, 2001; McDonald, 2002; Russell, 1999). In the 21st century, when the Internet is much more usable and the LMSs are more capable, advocates further insist that online learning can better support learners to learn effectively and to achieve their potential than before (Allen & Seaman, 2010; Harish, 2013; Ni, 2013).

It has to be confessed that advanced technology does bring a lot of benefits to online education. However, the learner is the center of instruction and learning, and education is a process of constructive interaction and convergent conceptual change (Koschmann, Myers, Feltovich, & Barrows, 1994; Vygotsky, 1978). Learners' interaction is the nature of the educational experience (Garrison & Cleveland-Innes, 2005).

DOI: 10.4324/b23163-1

Therefore, simply improving technology, making it available, and then requiring learners to use it does not necessarily guarantee successful learning experience in online settings (Larusson & White, 2014). There is a need, by employing new research methods, to investigate particular patterns and details of learners' interaction, especially in different groups of massive online learners.

The purpose of this book was to conduct data-driven research by employing learning analytics methodology and Big Data in LMSs, and then to identify and compare learners' interaction patterns in different achievement groups through different course processes in Massive Private Online Courses (MPOCs).

Learner interaction is the foundation of a successful online learning experience. However, the uncertainties about the temporal and sequential patterns of online interaction and the lack of knowledge about using dynamic interaction traces in LMSs have prevented research on ways to improve interactive qualities and learning effectiveness in online learning. Also, most research focuses on the most popular online learning organization form, Massive Open Online Courses (MOOCs), and little online learning research has been conducted to investigate learners' interaction behaviors in another important online learning organization form: MPOCs.

To fill these needs, the study pays attention to investigate the frequent and effective interaction patterns in different achievement groups as well as in different course processes, and attaches importance to LMS trace data (log data) in better serving learners and instructors in online learning. Further, the learning analytics methodology and techniques are introduced here into online interaction research.

We assume that learners with different achievements express different interaction characteristics. Therefore, the hypotheses in this study are: 1) the interaction activity patterns of the high-achievement group and the low-achievement group are different; 2) in both groups, interaction activity patterns evolve through different course processes (such as the learning process and the exam process). The final purpose is to find interaction activity patterns that characterize the different achievement groups in specific MPOCs courses.

Some learning analytics approaches, including Hidden Markov models (HMMs) and other related measures, are taken into account to identify frequently occurring interaction activity sequence patterns of High/Low achievement groups in the Learning/Exam processes under MPOCs settings. The results demonstrate that High-achievement learners especially focused on content learning, assignments, and quizzes to consolidate their knowledge construction in both Learning and Exam processes, while Low-achievement learners significantly did not perform the same. Further, High-achievement learners adjusted their learning strategies based on the goals of different course processes; Low-achievement learners were inactive in the learning process and opportunistic in the exam process. In addition, despite achievements or course processes, all learners were most interested in checking their performance statements, but they engaged little in forum discussion and group learning. In sum, the comparative analysis implies that certain interaction patterns may distinguish the High-achievement learners from the Low-achievement ones, and learners change their patterns more or less based on different course processes.

This study provides an attempt to conduct learner interaction research by employing learning analytics techniques. In the short term, the results will give in-depth knowledge of the dynamic interaction patterns of MPOCs learners. In the long term, the results will help learners gain insight into and evaluate their learning, help instructors identify at-risk learners and adjust instructional strategies, help developers and administrators to build recommendation systems based on objective and comprehensive information, all of which in turn will help improve the achievements of all learner groups in specific MPOC courses.

References

Allen, I. E., & Seaman, J. (2010). Class differences: Online education in the United States, 2010. *Sloan Consortium (NJ1)*, 30.

Allen, I. E., & Seaman, J. (2016). Online report card: Tracking online education in the United States. *Babson Survey Research Group*.

Allen, M., Bourhis, J., Burrell, N., & Mabry, E. (2002). Comparing student satisfaction with distance education to traditional classrooms in higher education: A meta-analysis. *The American Journal of Distance Education, 16*(2), 83–97.

Bernard, R. M., Abrami, P. C., Lou, Y., Borokhovski, E., Wade, A., Wozney, L., ... Huang, B. (2004). How does distance education compare with classroom instruction? A meta-analysis of the empirical literature. *Review of Educational Research, 74*(3), 379–439.

Browning, J. B. (1999). *Analysis of concepts and skills acquisition differences between Web-delivered and classroom-delivered undergraduate instructional technology courses*. (Doctoral dissertation), Retrieved from ProQuest Dissertations Publishing. (UMI No. 9938354)

Cavanaugh, C. S. (2001). The effectiveness of interactive distance education technologies in K-12 learning: A meta-analysis. *International Journal of Educational Telecommunications, 7*(1), 73.

Garrison, D. R., & Cleveland-Innes, M. (2005). Facilitating cognitive presence in online learning: Interaction is not enough. *The American Journal of Distance Education, 19*(3), 133–148.

Harish, J. (2013). Online education: A revolution in the making. *Cadmus, 2*(1), 26.

Inoue, Y., Ed. (2007). Online Education for Lifelong Learning. *Information Science Publishing, 8*(3), 341.

Kaplan, A. M., & Haenlein, M. (2016). Higher education and the digital revolution: About MOOCs, SPOCs, social media, and the Cookie Monster. *Business Horizons, 59*(4), 441–450. doi:10.1016/j.bushor.2016.03.008

Labaree, R. V. (2004). Issues in web based pedagogy: A critical primer (review). *Review of Higher Education, 27*(2), 280–281.

Larusson, J. A., & White, B. (2014). Introduction. In J. A. Larusson & B. White (Eds.), *Learning analytics: From research to practice* (pp. 1–12). New York, NY: Springer Science+Business Media.

McDonald, J. (2002). Is "as good as face-to-face" as good as it gets. *Journal of Asynchronous Learning Networks, 6*(2), 10–23.

Ni, A. Y. (2013). Comparing the effectiveness of classroom and online learning: Teaching research methods. *Journal of Public Affairs Education, 19*(2), 199–215.

Russell, T. L. (1999). *The no significant difference phenomenon: As reported in 355 research reports, summaries and papers*: North Carolina State University.

Snyder, T. D., de Brey, C., & Dillow, S. A. (2016). *Digest of education statistics 2014*. Washington, DC: National Center for Education Statistics, Institute of Education Sciences, U.S. Department of Education.

Wilson, B. G. (2004). Designing E-Learning environments for flexible activity and instruction. *Educational Technology Research and Development, 52*(4), 77–84. doi:10.1007/BF02504720

1 Online Learning Needs Learning Analytics

The Importance of Learner Interaction in Online Learning

Successful online learning depends on the collaborative efforts among institutions, administration, course designers, online instructors, online assistants, technical supporters, and other specialists (Clark & Mayer, 2016). However, learning is a process of interaction (Koschmann, Myers, Feltovich, & Barrows, 1994; Vygotsky, 1978).

Interaction is a significant foundation of successful online learning, and an important way to discover the laws of online learning (Billings, Connors, & Skiba, 2001; Hong, Lai, & Holton, 2003; Moore, 1989; Thurmond & Wambach, 2004; Wagner, 1994). Bates (1995) asserts that learners' high-quality interaction with learning content, instructors, and fellow students is essential for effective learning (Bates, 1995). How much benefits learners academically, socially, and affectively from online gain depends greatly on the quality of interaction with content, instructors, peers, and interface (Hillman, Willis, & Gunawardena, 1994; Moore, 1989). Especially, the characteristics, styles, patterns, and models of learners' online interaction are central and critical to successfully perform in online learning.

If institutions and providers do not grasp the characteristics of learner interaction, it is not easy for them to facilitate learners to have effective interaction with materials, instructors, and peers. Then, how could online learning be successful? Thus, there is a strong need to study the qualitative nature of online interaction, which will support high levels of learning (Garrison & Cleveland-Innes, 2005).

The Limitations of Traditional Interaction Research in Online Learning

As one of the pioneers and founders in distance education, Moore (1989) separated learner-centered interaction into three types: learner–content interaction, learner–instructor interaction, and learner–learner interaction (Moore, 1989). Further, Hillman and colleagues (1994) discussed another type: learner–interface interaction (the process of manipulating tools to

DOI: 10.4324/b23163-2

accomplish a task; it focuses on the access, skills, and attitudes necessary for successful technologically mediated learning) (Hillman et al., 1994).

Based on the literature, most of the previous research of online interaction is related to two streams: the factors that affect the four types of interaction, and the factors that are affected by the four types of interaction. Online interaction is the bridge to link these two streams; interaction is the center of the learning experience in online learning (Garrison & Cleveland-Innes, 2005; Koschmann, Myers, Feltovich, & Barrows, 1994; Moore, 1989; Vygotsky, 1978). Unfortunately, the previous research did not pay enough attention to investigate the details of online interaction itself. Learning is inherently a sequential process constructed by varieties of interaction (Chiu & Khoo, 2005), which can not be viewed as a sealed box. The sequential interaction events that happen repeatedly reveal the secret of how learning happens and why certain learning outcomes result (Compton-Lilly, 2013; Mercer, 2008).

Interaction trace data in LMSs is the real-time record for all the interaction behaviors, which is the cumulation of the 'lived experience' of online learners (Dringus, 2012). However, this experience is hidden behind the online media interface. In addition, the research methods of studying online interaction are still limited to traditional statistics and qualitative approaches, which are not appropriate to process large amounts of LMS trace data.

Advances in data measurement and research methods drive significant advances in scientific investigations (Molenaar, 2014). For example, the invention of microscope helped us observe and measure the details and processes that were previously unreachable, which resulted in great improvements in many research fields. Without fine-grained trace data and advanced research methods, it is not easy to identify the details of online learners' interaction, especially the patterns and characteristics in different online learner groups.

The Utility of Attaching Importance to LMS Log Data

Learning is a process of interaction, through which learners acquire meaningful skills and knowledge (Chen, 2004). However, in traditional face-to-face instruction, it is not convenient to collect and store the information of the interaction behavior, and it is not routine for researchers to trace and analyze such data. Thus, when online learning emerged as a new educational phenomenon, most researchers were still influenced by face-to-face instructional research and did not pay enough attention to the learner interaction trace recorded in LMSs.

Previously, technological stagnation has limited our ability to collect and measure fine-grained traces of learners in the learning process (Greene & Azevedo, 2010). Therefore, in traditional learning and instruction research, the concept of time and sequence of learning behaviors at the micro-level has not gained much attention. Most research often focuses on time nodes with long time spans, such as measuring data based on the timeline of pre-test and post-test. As such, it is not realistic for researchers to collect the details and changes in interaction behaviors occurring at the micro-level.

Currently, the development of technology and LMSs greatly supports researchers in gaining interaction traces of the learning process in online settings, which provides an opportunity to investigate the temporal and sequential characteristics of interaction (Molenaar, 2014; Reimann, 2009). In online learning, LMSs can capture and store large amounts of time-stamped learner interaction traces, such as the number and duration of online sessions, LMS tools accessed, messages read or posted, and content pages visited (Macfadyen & Dawson, 2010). These time-stamped and sequential interaction traces accumulated by LMSs are generally called log data (aka 'Big Data'). Log data is captured in real time and can be mined at any stage of online course progression (Bomatpalli, 2014).

Different learners conduct learning process with different interaction characteristics (Chen, 2004). One of the beliefs in this study is that certain interaction patterns may distinguish the high-achievement groups from the low-achievement ones. Why do some learners earn the high achievement, while others earn low achievement? Do different achievement groups conduct interaction differently throughout the whole learning process? What are the general interaction patterns of different achievement groups? Do learner interaction states change at different course processes? Although online learners' lived experience is hidden behind the online media interface, it does need to be visualized and interpreted.

The comparison and interpretation of interaction patterns of different achievement groups may be useful to improve the understanding of learners' learning, predict the achievement of learning outcomes, and inform support interventions on course design and resource allocation. It may be a new way to understand the secret of learning and then to improve the learning achievements of all the learners in online settings. In fact, a steadily growing group of researchers is interested in the questions that address how different interaction behaviors develop over time (Molenaar, 2014). With this growing focus on investigating the temporal and sequential characteristics of interaction in online learning, the analysis and interpretation of interaction patterns over time are becoming more necessary.

Unfortunately, traditional statistical methods are not currently sufficient and effective in mining valuable interaction patterns from the sequential, meaningful, but massive log data in online learning. Without effective methods to decode the secret of the fine-grained log data in LMSs, it is completely unrealistic to deepen learner interaction research in online learning.

The Need for Applying Academically Sound Methods to Investigate Interaction Patterns

Data and methods are complementary to each other (Pistilli, Willis III, & Campbell, 2014). To investigate the effective interaction sequence patterns with MPOCs data, several questions have to be answered: What methods for analysis are available? What does a method of analysis even look like? What is the unit of analysis? How can researchers effectively organize log data? How does this information enrich learners' learning experiences? (Larusson & White, 2014). Traditional statistical methodology can neither well manipulate sequential log data nor precisely answer these important questions (Gibson & Ifenthaler, 2017).

The goal of traditional statistics is to infer population parameters from small samples (Behrens & DiCerbo, 2014). Null hypothesis significance testing (NHST) is the most common strategy in statistical quantitative analysis. However, the logic of NHST is based on questions including whether there is a significant effect or not, and whether to support or discredit a priori speculations about some aspect of a population (Gibson & Ifenthaler, 2017). Therefore, it is hard to detect what ways data are related within what structures, and with what specific predictable bounded as well as changing sequences and sets of relationships (Gibson & Ifenthaler, 2017). However, in this study, the characteristics of log data and the research focuses are closely related to time sequence interaction traces, which means structures, relationships, and sequences of data are the primary consideration when selecting the appropriate research methods.

Fortunately, the emergence of a new methodology, learning analytics, has the potential to unlock the value of LMS log data (Macfadyen & Dawson, 2010). It is a data-driven process and emphasizes converting educational data into useful actions to foster learning (Chatti, Muslim, & Schroeder, 2017). Learning analytics focuses on analyzing and detecting patterns within data sets, which provides a window into what actually takes place over the whole process when learners interact online (Larusson & White, 2014). In learning analytics, mining temporal and sequential pattern is the key to unlock the secret of learner interaction online (Baker & Inventado, 2016).

To determine the most frequent, effective interaction sequences is one of the goals of learning analytics (Macfadyen, Dawson, Pardo, & Gaševic, 2014), which is also the purpose of this study.

The Paucity of Learner Interaction Research in MPOCs

Given the differences in providers, course structures and goals, there are different organization forms for institutions to manage learners in online learning, which produce different characteristics of LMS log data. The two widely known forms in online learning are MOOCs, which means massive open online courses and SPOCs, which means small private online courses: these two forms differ primarily in the sizes of the learner populations to which they cater (Kaplan & Haenlein, 2016).

However, another important form, MPOCs, has been less discussed by researchers. An MPOC is a massive private online course designed on the model of SPOC in conventional online learning settings. MPOCs also offer a limited size of enrollment like SPOCs, but the size of online classes in MPOCs is big and the number of learners is massive. One example of MPOCs is a training program with 500,000 participants in about 5,000 online classes at Peking University in China (Guo, 2014). MPOCs produce rich, regulated, complete, and centralized data full of interaction details through uninterrupted semesters, such as interaction patterns, engagement, and degree and mode of participation in online settings (Dawson, McWilliam, & Tan, 2008). Further, most MPOCs cannot only accumulate relatively complete interaction data but also collect the learners' demographic data and prior academic data (Guo, 2014).

Given the extremely high dropout rate in MOOCs (Hew & Cheung, 2014; Khalil & Ebner, 2014; Koller, Ng, Do, & Chen, 2013) and small sizes of participants in SPOCs, MPOCs with high retention and formal organization may provide a more complete picture of learner interaction in online settings. In addition, learners in MPOCs are more engaged, active, persistent, and goal-oriented, and therefore, their learning is more active and effective (Guo, 2014). Thus, researchers and organizations in online learning do not need to spend a lot of time on questions regarding retention or persistence; rather, the focus in MPOCs is directly to help as many as possible learners to facilitate their learning, improve effectiveness and achieve final learning purposes. Unfortunately, MOOCs have been the research hotspot in recent years, and less attention has been paid to MPOCs (Perna et al., 2014).

In recent years, there have been some studies focusing on online interaction behaviors. But these studies were conducted with experimental or quasi-experimental conditions with few participants and a short time span. The data are from learners in primary schools, high schools, colleges, especially in MOOCs. The educational environments include collaborative learning, self-regulated learning, game-based learning, or concept mapping activities. However, none of these studies has tried to extract interaction patterns in MPOCs, in which interaction behaviors happen in daily online courses, supporting massive learners with regular learning behaviors through an entire semester in MPOCs settings. That is because the massive online learners, long-term learning process, non-experimental environment, and huge data together present big challenges for researchers to analyze fine-grained interaction behaviors at the micro-level.

Therefore, to overcome this limitation, this study aims to find interaction patterns that can distinguish learners based on their interaction activities/ actions in MPOCs settings. By employing learning analytics approaches, this study identifies the interaction behavior patterns at the activity level and compares patterns between different achievement groups in different course processes. Also, this study validates a set of theoretical assumptions in the research area of learning interaction and tests the effectiveness and stability of some learning analytics techniques.

Definition of Key Terms

LMS: Learning Management System (LMS) is a set of digital services commonly used in online learning and blended learning to plan, implement, and assess specific learning processes, such as launch learning content, keep track of learner progress, sequence learning objects, and report learners' performances (Graf, Liu, & Kinshuk, 2010; Psaromiligkos, Orfanidou, Kytagias, & Zafiri, 2011).

Moodle: Moodle is a free open source course management system designed to help educators create effective online learning communities, which has a flexible array of course activities such as forums, chats, quizzes, resources, choices, surveys, or assignments (Romero, González, Ventura, Del Jesús, & Herrera, 2009). The activities allowed by Moodle are mostly interactions between instructors and learners, among learners, and between learners and contents (Park, Yu, & Jo, 2016).

MOOC: An MOOC is an open-access online course (i.e., without specific participation restrictions) that allows for unlimited (massive) participation; many MOOCs provide interactive elements to encourage interactions among learners and between learners and the teaching staff, although the latter is not a defining requirement (Kaplan & Haenlein, 2016).

MPOC: An MPOC is a massive private online course, which requires some form of formal enrollment with a competitive application process and charges a tuition fee in conventional online learning settings; the tuition in MPOCs is low, the size of online classes in MPOCs is big, and the number of learners is massive (Guo, 2014).

Log data: In online learning, large amounts of time-stamped learner behaviors captured and stored in LMSs are generally called log data, such as the number and duration of online sessions, LMS tools accessed, messages read or posted, and content pages visited, which is the foundation of big data in education (Macfadyen & Dawson, 2010).

Learning analytics: The measurement, collection, analysis, and reporting of data about learners and their contexts, for purposes of understanding and optimizing learning and the environments in which it occurs (Siemens & Long, 2011).

Interaction activity: In this study, an interaction activity is defined as a sequence of learner interaction behaviors within one LMS module with learning and instructional meanings. For example, in Moodle, corresponding to the modules, interaction activities may include Introduction, Content, Forum, Quiz, Assignment, and so on.

Interaction action: This is defined as the educationally meaningful typical behavior in an interaction activity such as view, delete, change, create, and so on.

Interaction pattern: Learning is an 'inherently sequential' process consisting of interaction behaviors, which cannot be viewed as a series of discrete activities (Chiu & Khoo, 2005). The temporal dimension of interaction can help reveal the secret of learners' thinking progression (Compton-Lilly, 2013). A set of specific interaction events that repeatedly happen is defined as an interaction pattern. It can help the researcher decode how learning happens and why certain learning outcomes result (Mercer, 2008).

References

Baker, R., & Inventado, P. S. (2016). Educational data mining and learning analytics: Potentials and possibilities for online education. In G. Veletsianos (Ed.), *Emergence and innovation in digital learning: Foundations and applications* (pp. 83–98). Edmonton, AB, Canada: Athabasca University Press.
Bates, A. W. (1995). *Technology, open learning and distance education.* New York, NY: Routledge.
Behrens, J. T., & DiCerbo, K. E. (2014). Harnessing the currents of the digital ocean. In J. A. Larusson & B. White (Eds.), *Learning analytics: From research to practice* (pp. 39–60). New York, NY: Springer Science+Business Media.
Billings, D. M., Connors, H. R., & Skiba, D. J. (2001). Benchmarking best practices in web-based nursing courses. *Advances in Nursing Science, 23*(3), 41–52.
Bomatpalli, T. (2014). Learning analytics and big data in higher education. *International Journal of Engineering Research & Technology, 3*(1), 3377–3383.
Chatti, M. A., Muslim, A., & Schroeder, U. (2017). Toward an open Learning Analytics ecosystem. In B. K. Daniel (Ed.), *Big data and learning analytics in higher education* (pp. 195–219). Switzerland: Springer International Publishing.
Chen, L. (2004). An investigation into "Interactivity" and the related concepts. *China Distance Education, 3*, 12–19.
Chiu, M., & Khoo, L. (2005). A new method for analyzing sequential processes: Dynamic multi-level analysis. *Small Group Research, 36*, 600–631. doi:10.1177/1046496405279309
Clark, R. C., & Mayer, R. E. (2016). *E-learning and the science of instruction.* Hobaken, NJ: John Wiley & Sons, Inc.
Compton-Lilly, C. (2013). Temporal discourse analysis. In T. Holbrook, P. Albers, & A. F. Routledge (Eds.), *New methods on literacy research* (pp. 40–55). London, UK: Routledge.
Dawson, S. P., McWilliam, E., & Tan, J. P.-L. (2008). Teaching smarter: How mining ICT data can inform and improve learning and teaching practice. http://www.ascilite.org.au/conferences/melbourne08/procs/dawson.pdf
Dringus, L. P. (2012). Learning analytics considered harmful. *Journal of Asynchronous Learning Networks, 16*(3), 87–100.
Garrison, D. R., & Cleveland-Innes, M. (2005). Facilitating cognitive presence in online learning: Interaction is not enough. *The American Journal of Distance Education, 19*(3), 133–148.
Gibson, D., & Ifenthaler, D. (2017). Preparing the next generation of education researchers for big data in higher education. In B. K. Daniel (Ed.), *Big data and learning analytics in higher education* (pp. 29–42). Switzerland: Springer International Publishing.
Graf, S., Liu, T.-C., & Kinshuk. (2010). Analysis of learners' navigational behaviour and their learning styles in an online course. *Journal of Computer Assisted Learning, 26*(2), 116–131. doi:10.1111/j.1365-2729.2009.00336.x

Greene, J. A., & Azevedo, R. (2010). The measurement of learners' self-regulated cognitive and metacognitive processes while using computer-based learning environments. *Educational Psychologist, 45*(4), 203–209.

Guo, W. (2014, October). *From SPOC to MPOC--The effective practice of Peking University online teacher training*. Paper presented at the International Conference of Educational Innovation through Technology, Queensland, Australia.

Hew, K. F., & Cheung, W. S. (2014). Students' and instructors' use of massive open online courses (MOOCs): Motivations and challenges. *Educational Research Review, 12*, 45–58. doi:10.1016/j.edurev.2014.05.001

Hillman, D. C., Willis, D. J., & Gunawardena, C. N. (1994). Learner-interface interaction in distance education: An extension of contemporary models and strategies for practitioners. *American Journal of Distance Education, 8*(2), 30–42.

Hong, K.-S., Lai, K.-W., & Holton, D. (2003). Students' satisfaction and perceived learning with a web-based course. *Educational Technology & Society, 6*(1), 116–124.

Kaplan, A. M., & Haenlein, M. (2016). Higher education and the digital revolution: About MOOCs, SPOCs, social media, and the Cookie Monster. *Business Horizons, 59*(4), 441–450. doi:10.1016/j.bushor.2016.03.008

Khalil, H., & Ebner, M. (2014, June). *MOOCs completion rates and possible methods to improve retention - A literature review*. Paper presented at the EdMedia: World Conference on Educational Multimedia, Hypermedia and Telecommunications, Tampere, Finland.

Koller, D., Ng, A., Do, C., & Chen, Z. (2013). Retention and intention in Massive Open Online Courses. *EDUCAUSE Review, 48*(3), 62.

Koschmann, T. D., Myers, A. C., Feltovich, P. J., & Barrows, H. S. (1994). Using technology to assist in realizing effective learning and instruction: A principled approach to the use of computers in collaborative learning. *Journal of the Learning Sciences, 3*(3), 227–264.

Larusson, J. A., & White, B. (2014). Introduction. In J. A. Larusson & B. White (Eds.), *Learning analytics: From research to practice* (pp. 1–12). New York, NY: Springer Science+Business Media.

Macfadyen, L. P., & Dawson, S. (2010). Mining LMS data to develop an "early warning system" for educators: A proof of concept. *Computers & Education, 54*(2), 588–599.

Macfadyen, L. P., Dawson, S., Pardo, A., & Gašević, D. (2014). Embracing big data in complex educational systems: The learning analytics imperative and the policy challenge. *Research & Practice in Assessment, 9*, 17–28.

Mercer, N. (2008). The seeds of time: Why classroom dialogue needs a temporal analysis. *Journal of the Learning Sciences, 17*(1), 33–59.

Molenaar, I. (2014). Advances in temporal analysis in learning and instruction. *Frontline Learning Research, 2*(4), 15–24.

Moore, M. G. (1989). Editorial: Three types of interaction. *The American Journal of Distance Education, 3*(2), 1–6.

Park, Y., Yu, J. H., & Jo, I.-H. (2016). Clustering blended learning courses by online behavior data: A case study in a Korean higher education institute. *The Internet and Higher Education, 29*, 1–11.

Perna, L. W., Ruby, A., Boruch, R. F., Wang, N., Scull, J., Ahmad, S., & Evans, C. (2014). Moving through MOOCs: Understanding the progression of users in massive open online courses. *Educational Researcher, 43*(9), 421–432.

Pistilli, M. D., Willis III, J. E., & Campbell, J. P. (2014). Analytics through an institutional lens: Definition, theory, design, and impact. In J. A. Larusson & B. White (Eds.), *Learning analytics: From research to practice* (pp. 79–102). New York, NY: Springer Science+Business Media.

Psaromiligkos, Y., Orfanidou, M., Kytagias, C., & Zafiri, E. (2011). Mining log data for the analysis of learners' behaviour in web-based learning management systems. *Operational Research, 11*(2), 187–200.

Reimann, P. (2009). Time is precious: Variable- and event-centred approaches to process analysis in CSCL research. *International Journal of Computer-Supported Collaborative Learning, 4*(3), 239–257. doi:10.1007/s11412-009-9070-z

Romero, C., González, P., Ventura, S., Del Jesús, M. J., & Herrera, F. (2009). Evolutionary algorithms for subgroup discovery in e-learning: A practical application using Moodle data. *Expert Systems with Applications, 36*(2), 1632–1644.

Siemens, G., & Long, P. (2011). Penetrating the fog: Analytics in learning and education. *EDUCAUSE Review, 46*(4), 31–40.

Thurmond, V. A., & Wambach, K. (2004). Understanding interactions in distance education: A review of the literature. *International Journal of Instructional Technology and Distance Learning, 1*(1), 9–26.

Vygotsky, L. S. (1978). *Mind in society: The development of higher psychological processes* (M. Cole, V. John-Steiner, S. Schribner, & E. Souberman, Trans. M. Cole, V. John-Steiner, S. Schribner, & E. Souberman Eds.). Cambridge, MA: Harvard University Press.

Wagner, E. D. (1994). In support of a functional definition of interaction. *American Journal of Distance Education, 8*(2), 6–29.

2 Traditional Learner Interaction Research in Online Learning

Online Learner Interaction Theory

The foundational theory helpful to investigate interaction in online learning is Moore's transactional distance theory (Moore & Kearsley, 1996). In this theory, Moore postulated that distance is a pedagogical phenomenon, rather than a function of geographic separation; and he identified learner interactions by entities involved in each exchange: learner–content interaction, learner–instructor interaction, and learner–learner interaction (Woods & Baker, 2004). Although other types of interaction are often addressed by researchers from different perspectives; Moore's three types are the most common and durable interaction types accepted by educators, researchers, and online learning participants (Northrup, Lee, & Burgess, 2002; Pham, University, & Dakich, 2014).

Learner–Content Interaction

Moore (1989) described it as 'the process of intellectually interacting with the content that results in changes in the learner's understanding, the learner's perspective, or the cognitive structures of the learner's mind' (Moore, 1989, p. 2). A variation of learner–content interaction is learner–self interaction, which examines the learner's reaction to the content and asserts that their reflections and inner-dialogue (called 'self-talk') are related to the learning process (Soo & Bonk, 1998). Another variation is learner–information interaction (Sabry & Baldwin, 2003), which accounts for information specific to the course material as well as information relevant to the learning task but not specific to the content, such as learning how to conduct a Web search when creating a Webquest about something (Wanstreet, 2006).

Learner–Instructor Interaction

It refers to two-way communication between the instructor and learners in the course (Moore & Kearsley, 1996). The instructor seeks 'to stimulate or at least maintain the student's interest in what is to be taught, to motivate the student to learn, to enhance and maintain the learner's interest, including self-direction and self-motivation' (Moore, 1989, p. 2). Learner–instructor interaction may be synchronous such as through the telephone, videoconferencing, and chats, or asynchronous such as through correspondence, e-mail, and discussion boards (Abrami, Bernard, Bures, Borokhovski, & Tamim, 2011).

Learner–Learner Interaction

It involves a two-way reciprocal communication among learners, with or without the presence of an instructor (Moore, 1989). This type of interaction encourages experimentation, sharing of ideas, increased and more distributed participation, and collaborative thinking (Bouhnik & Marcus, 2006; Jonassen & Kwon, 2001; Trentin, 1998). Engaging in peer interaction propels learners to construct ideas deeply, gain social and emotional support, and increases achievement (Anderson, 2003; Haythornthwaite, 2001).

Learner–Interface Interaction

Though Moore's (1989) theory of interaction can be applied to both face-to-face and online environments, most research using the framework has been related to online learning. To address the particular concerns in online learning, scholars began to revisit the original interaction theory and additional dimensions of interaction were introduced (Northrup et al., 2002; Pham et al., 2014). Hillman, Willis, and Gunawardena (1994) proposed a new dimension of interaction: learner–interface interaction, which is the interaction that takes place between a learner and the technology used to mediate a particular online learning process; the mediation technology may include specific technologies, platforms, applications, and course templates to interact with course content, instructors, and classmates (Hillman, Willis, & Gunawardena, 1994; Lehtinen, 2002; Wanstreet, 2006).

Later in 2003, Thurmond summed up the essence of previous research and defined the concept of learner interaction in online learning (Thurmond, 2003). He clarified learner interaction as '… the learner's engagement with the course content, other learners, the instructor, and the technological medium used in the course. True interactions with other learners, the instructor, and the technology results in a reciprocal exchange of information. The exchange of information is intended to enhance knowledge development in the learning environment. … Ultimately, the goal of the interaction is to increase understanding of the course content or mastery of the defined goals' (Thurmond, 2003, p. 4).

Traditional Research on Online Interaction

Research Related to Learner–Content Interaction

Interaction plays a critical role in the learning process. In online learning, interaction with the course content (learner–content interaction) is especially important because it can contribute to successful learning outcomes and course completion (Zimmerman, 2012). Thus, many researchers put their sights on the factors influencing learner–content interaction.

Leasure and colleagues (2000) found that self-direction of learners can influence their interaction with course content (Leasure, Davis, & Thievon, 2000). They conducted quantitative research to compare learner outcomes in an undergraduate research course taught using both online learning and traditional teaching. The results showed that learners who reported that they were self-directed and had the ability to maintain their own pace and avoid procrastination were most suited to online learning (Leasure et al., 2000). Online discussion is also helpful for learner–content interaction, Swan (2001) found that active discussion among learners can help learners perceive greater learning. In online discussions, learners refine the learning content by communicating with others in the discussions (Swan, 2001). Lack of time to participate in course work has been identified as a barrier to learner content interaction (Atack & Rankin, 2002). The learners who did not have time to access the content at work indicated that their work environment probably was not an ideal environment for learner–content interactions (Atack & Rankin, 2002). Reisetter, LaPointe, and Korcuska (2007) focused on the online experiences of graduate learners. Learners perceived that course materials such as the learner–content variables were mediated through the teacher's organization and presentations (Reisetter, LaPointe, & Korcuska, 2007).

Information presented in multiple forms is also an important factor influencing learner–content interaction (Clark & Mayer, 2016; Park & Etgen, 2000). In addition, Zhang (2005) conducted an empirical study, which revealed that when a multimedia e-learning environment offered more learner–content interaction, learning performance and learner satisfaction could be improved. The multimedia includes the forms such as video + slides, video + slides + lecture notes, audio + slides, and slides + lecture notes (Zhang, 2005).

On the other hand, some researchers focus on the influences of learner–content interaction. Thurmond and Wambach (2004) pointed out that when learners have more continuous interaction with the content in a Web-based course, this may contribute to more learning and overall greater satisfaction with the course (Thurmond & Wambach, 2004). Swan (2001) found that clarity of design significantly influenced learners' satisfaction and perceived learning. If learning content is presented using a similar format, it is easier for learners to perceive learning (Swan, 2001). Zimmerman (2012) examined the relationship between learner–content interaction and course grade to determine if this interaction type is a contributing success factor. The study concluded that learners who spent more time interacting with course content achieve higher grades than those who spent less time with the content (Zimmerman, 2012).

Research Related to Learner–Instructor Interaction

Many studies indicated that learners agreed that timely, prompt feedback from their instructor contributed to positive perceptions of learner–instructor interactions (Thurmond, 2003; Vrasidas & McIsaac, 1999).

Sargeant and colleagues (2006) used a purposive sampling method to conduct a qualitative study to explore instructor roles in enhancing online learning through interpersonal interaction. They suggested that instructors require enhanced skills to engage learners in meaningful interaction and to overcome the transactional distance of online learning (Sargeant, Curran, Allen, Jarvis-Selinger, & Ho, 2006). Muhirwa (2009) found multiple obstacles to quality learner–instructor interaction, including lack of instructor presence, ill-prepared local tutors, poor social dynamics, learner–learner conflict, learner–instructor conflict, and learner withdrawal and resignation (Muhirwa, 2009). Skog (2010) summarized several important components that are important to learner–instructor interaction: discussions where the teacher also comments, not just the learners; meaningful instructor comments and feedback; good discussion prompts; and allowing discussions to facilitate the needs of the learners (Skog, 2010).

On the other side, learner-instructor interaction impacts greatly on learners' performance and satisfaction. There is a positive relationship between the amount of learner interaction with the instructor and learners' level of perceived learning (Fredericksen, Pickett, Shea, Pelz, & Swan, 2000). Additionally, learners perceived more interaction with their instructor the more their course grade depended on their participation (Swan, 2001). Dennen and colleagues (2007) reported that learner performance is more likely tied to instructor actions that are focused on course content and provide both proactive (models, expectations) and reactive (feedback) information to learners about their ability to demonstrate knowledge of course material (Dennen, Aubteen Darabi, & Smith, 2007). Kang and Im (2013) found factors such as instructional communication, instructional support and management of learning materials, guidance and facilitating learning, and presence of instructors can predict the learner's outcomes in the online learning environment. These instructor behaviors also predicted students' perceived learning achievement and satisfaction better than factors related to social interaction. (Kang & Im, 2013).

Research Related to Learner–Learner Interaction

Findings regarding learner–learner interaction indicated that learners who interacted more in online learning may perceive greater learning. Also, teamwork or collaborative learning is the most general form of learner–learner interaction, which is intended to promote understanding the course content and stimulate critical thinking (Hay, Hodgkinson, Peltier, & Drago, 2004; Palloff & Pratt, 2002). Smyth (2011) presented a model that distinguishes between planned learner-content interaction and learner–learner interaction. The results suggested that a blend of planned and non-planned learner-learner interaction is worthwhile (Smyth, 2011). Online discussion is the most general learner–learner interaction in online learning, which is because of its relation to the development of participatory citizenship, critical thinking, and community (Huang, 2014; Larson & Keiper, 2002).

Research Related to Learner–Interface Interaction

Sinha, Khreisat, and Sharma (2009) described how learner–interface interaction promotes active learning. Results indicated that technologies facilitate the creation of a non-threatening, flexible, and challenging learning environment (Sinha, Khreisat, & Sharma, 2009).

Jung and colleagues (2002) empirically tested learner–interface interaction in an online course. The study investigated the effect that online settings had on the learners' satisfaction, participation, and attitude towards online learning (Jung, Choi, Lim, & Leem, 2002). Researchers asserted that learner–interface interaction would help learners in deep and meaningful learner–content interactions (Zimmerman, 2012).

On the other hand, there are also many factors that impact on learner–interface interaction in online learning. Learners' experiences with information technology can affect their online learning (Leasure et al., 2000) and improve their technology skills (Atack & Rankin, 2002). Learners' perception regarding technology also impacts on learner–interface interaction (Daley et al., 2001).

In addition, Swan (2004) studied the effects of course interfaces on learner learning in the online environment. It shows that particular media and combinations of media are more supportive of online learning than others, as are specific instructional sequences and particular navigational interfaces (Swan, 2004). Muhirwa (2009) found obstacles to quality learner–interface interaction which include frequent Internet disconnections, limited learner access to computers, learner unfamiliarity with typing and computer technology, and ineffective technical support (Muhirwa, 2009).

Discussion

Most studies mentioned above are before and around 2010, which ranged over a variety of topics related to the four traditional types of learner interaction in online learning. The literature revealed two main streams of thought related to how researchers conduct learner interaction research in online learning.

In the first stream, researchers have paid much attention to identifying factors that affect each particular type of learner interaction. Such factors could be called 'factors affecting interaction'. Different factors impact differently on four types of learner interaction. Factors such as self-direction, online discussion, time constraints, and information presented in multiple forms influence learner–content interaction. A comfortable learning environment, instructor actions relative to course content, guidance and promptness in discussions, interpersonal communication with a learner, individualized corrective feedback, and support of learning materials management influence learner-instructor interaction. Social isolation, collaboration, a blend of planned and non-planned interaction, and online discussion influence learner–learner interaction. Finally, computer experience, learner perception regarding technology, inconvenience and poor accessing of content, technology obstacles, and interface navigation influence learner–interface interaction.

In the second stream, researchers have focused on factors affected by a different type of learner interaction, which can be called 'factors being affected by interaction'. Generally, the four types of learner interaction impact greatly on the satisfaction, quality, retention, performance and final achievement of learners' online learning (Kuo, Walker, Belland, & Schroder, 2014).

It has to be confessed that the two research streams clarify the logical line from 'factors affecting interaction' to learner interaction to 'factors being affected by interaction', which strongly supports the belief from many scholars that interaction is the center of learning experience in online learning (Garrison & Cleveland-Innes, 2005; Koschmann, Myers, Feltovich, & Barrows, 1994; Moore, 1989; Vygotsky, 1978).

Unfortunately, these two streams related to learner interaction in online learning, no matter whether factors affecting learner interaction or factors affected by learner interaction, did not focus on learner interaction itself. In other words, most of the studies did not investigate learners' interaction behavior at a micro-level. Thus, such studies can not answer questions such as: Are there sequential patterns of learner interaction in online learning? Do different achievement groups conduct interaction differently? Do learners' interaction patterns change with different course processes?

The learner is the center of education, and constructive learner interaction has been discussed as the nature of learning and a primary focus in the study of online learning (Chen, 2004; Garrison & Cleveland-Innes, 2005; Koschmann et al., 1994; Moore, 1989; Vygotsky, 1978; Zimmerman, 2012). Such opinions reflect the fundamental principles generally accepted in today's educational area, especially in online learning. However, if we do not know how learners, in real time, conduct their interaction at the micro-level, how could we identify effective interaction patterns from high-achievement groups as well as weak patterns from low-achievement groups? How could we clarify the changes in interaction patterns in different course processes?

How could we facilitate learners to achieve the final goals of online courses, and improve learner's performance in essence? Therefore, this study focuses on learner interaction itself and aims to decode the secret of how learners interact in online learning.

The necessary precondition for identifying the interaction details of learners' in online settings is to find useful sources of data recording the information of interaction in real time. However, based on the literature above, the data in previous studies were typically collected from learners' course grades or scores, evaluations of performance based on learning goals, self-reported surveys/questionnaires, or interviews, all of which are not closely related to the details of interaction in real time. Further, most of the researchers employed traditional quantitative methods (statistics) and qualitative methods to analyze the data and conduct their research. Therefore, to focus on the interaction itself and investigate interaction patterns in online learning, data indicating temporal and sequential interaction traces is really needed. Fortunately, LMSs provide abundant data with all the sequential information of learner interaction in real time. The prior task of taking advantage of the rich data from LMSs is to know the foundation of data in LMSs: log data.

References

Abrami, P. C., Bernard, R. M., Bures, E. M., Borokhovski, E., & Tamim, R. M. (2011). Interaction in distance education and online learning: Using evidence and theory to improve practice. *Journal of Computing in Higher Education, 23*(2-3), 82–103.

Anderson, T. (2003). Getting the mix right again: An updated and theoretical rationale for interaction. *International Review of Research in Open & Distance Learning, 4*(2), 65-65.

Atack, L., & Rankin, J. (2002). A descriptive study of registered nurses' experiences with web-based learning. *Journal of Advanced Nursing, 40,* 457–465.

Bouhnik, D., & Marcus, T. (2006). Interaction in distance-learning courses. *Journal of the American Society for Information Science and Technology, 57*(3), 299–305.

Chen, L. (2004). An investigation into "Interactivity" and the related concepts. *China Distance Education, 3,* 12–19.

Clark, R. C., & Mayer, R. E. (2016). *E-learning and the science of instruction.* Hoboken, NJ: John Wiley & Sons, Inc.

Daley, B. J., Watkins, K., Williams, S. W., Courtenay, B., Davis, M., & Dymock, D. (2001). Exploring learning in a technology-enhanced environment. *Journal of Educational Technology & Society, 4*(3), 126–138.

Dennen, V. P., Aubteen Darabi, A., & Smith, L. J. (2007). Instructor–learner interaction in online courses: The relative perceived importance of particular instructor actions on performance and satisfaction. *Distance Education, 28*(1), 65–79.

Fredericksen, E., Pickett, A., Shea, P., Pelz, W., & Swan, K. (2000). Student satisfaction and perceived learning with online courses-principles and examples from the SUNY learning network. *Journal of Asynchronous Learning Networks, 4*(2), 7–41.

Garrison, D. R., & Cleveland-Innes, M. (2005). Facilitating cognitive presence in online learning: Interaction is not enough. *The American Journal of Distance Education, 19*(3), 133–148.

Hay, A., Hodgkinson, M., Peltier, J. W., & Drago, W. A. (2004). Interaction and virtual learning. *Strategic Change, 13*(4), 193–204.

Haythornthwaite, C. (2001). Exploring Multiplexity: Social Network Structures in a computer-supported distance learning class. *Information Society, 17*(3), 211–226.

Hillman, D. C., Willis, D. J., & Gunawardena, C. N. (1994). Learner-interface interaction in distance education: An extension of contemporary models and strategies for practitioners. *American Journal of Distance Education, 8*(2), 30–42.

Huang, Y. (2014). *Structuring asynchronous online discussion groups: The impact of role-supported student facilitation*. (Ph.D. Dissertation), University of Missouri--Columbia, University of Missouri Library Systems. Retrieved from https://hdl.handle.net/10355/48212

Jonassen, D. H., & Kwon, H. (2001). Communication patterns in computer mediated versus face-to-face group problem solving. *Educational Technology Research & Development, 49*(1), 35–51.

Jung, I., Choi, S., Lim, C., & Leem, J. (2002). Effects of different types of interaction on learning achievement, satisfaction and participation in web-based instruction. *Innovations in Education and Teaching International, 39*(2), 153–162.

Kang, M., & Im, T. (2013). Factors of learner–instructor interaction which predict perceived learning outcomes in online learning environment. *Journal of Computer Assisted Learning, 29*(3), 292–301. doi: 10.1111/jcal.12005

Koschmann, T. D., Myers, A. C., Feltovich, P. J., & Barrows, H. S. (1994). Using technology to assist in realizing effective learning and instruction: A principled approach to the use of computers in collaborative learning. *Journal of the Learning Sciences, 3*(3), 227–264.

Kuo, Y. C., Walker, A., Belland, B. R., & Schroder, K. E. E. (2014). A case study of integrating interwise: Interaction, internet self-efficacy, and satisfaction in synchronous online learning environments. *International Review of Research in Open & Distance Learning, 15*(1), 161–181.

Larson, B. E., & Keiper, T. A. (2002). Classroom discussion and threaded electronic discussion: Learning in two arenas. *Contemporary Issues in Technology and Teacher Education, 2*(1), 45–62.

Leasure, A. R., Davis, L., & Thievon, S. L. (2000). Comparison of student outcomes and preferences in a traditional vs. world wide web-based baccalaureate nursing research course. *Journal of Nursing Education, 39*(4), 149–154.

Lehtinen, E. (2002). Developing models for distributed problem-based learning: Theoretical and methodological reflection. *Distance Education, 23*(1), 109–117.

Moore, M. G. (1989). Editorial: Three types of interaction. *The American Journal of Distance Education, 3*(2), 1–6.

Moore, M. G., & Kearsley, G. (1996). *Distance education: A system view*. Belmont: Wadsworth Publishing Company.

Muhirwa, J.-M. (2009). Teaching and learning against all odds: A video-based study of learner-to-instructor interaction in international distance education. *The International Review of Research in Open and Distributed Learning, 10*(4).

Northrup, P., Lee, R., & Burgess, V. (2002). *Learner perceptions of online interaction*. Paper presented at the ED-MEDIA 2002 World Conference on Educational Multimedia, Hypermedia & Telecommunications, Denver, CO.

Palloff, R. M., & Pratt, K. (2002). *Lessons from the cyberspace classroom: The realities of online teaching*: John Wiley & Sons.

Park, O. C., & Etgen, M. P. (2000). Research-based principles for multimedia presentation. In J. M. Spector & T. M. Anderson (Eds.), *Integrated and holistic perspectives on learning instruction and technology* (pp. 197–212). London: Kluwer.

Pham, T., University, V., & Dakich, E. (2014). Frequency and pattern of learner-instructor interaction in an online English language learning environment in Vietnam. *Australasian Journal of Educational Technology, 30*(6), 686–698.

Reisetter, M., LaPointe, L., & Korcuska, J. (2007). The impact of altered realties: Implications of online delivery for learners' interactions, expectations, and learning skills. *International Journal on ELearning, 6*(1), 55.

Sabry, K., & Baldwin, L. (2003). Web-based learning interaction and learning styles. *British Journal of Educational Technology, 34*(4), 443–454.

Sargeant, J., Curran, V., Allen, M., Jarvis-Selinger, S., & Ho, K. (2006). Facilitating interpersonal interaction and learning online: Linking theory and practice. *The Journal of Continuing Education in the Health Professions, 26*(2), 128–136.

Sinha, N., Khreisat, L., & Sharma, K. (2009). Learner-interface interaction for technology-enhanced active learning. *Innovate Journal of Online Education, 5*(3), 1–7.

Skog, T. K. (2010). Learner satisfaction in online learning. *Quarterly Review of Distance Education, 8*(3), 192–193.

Smyth, R. (2011). Enhancing learner–learner interaction using video communications in higher education: Implications from theorising about a new model. *British Journal of Educational Technology, 42*(1), 113–127.

Soo, K.-S., & Bonk, C. J. (1998). Interaction: what does it mean in online distance education? Retrieved from https://eric.ed.gov/?id=ED428724

Swan, K. (2001). Virtual interaction: Design factors affecting student satisfaction and perceived learning in asynchronous online courses. *Distance Education, 22*, 306–331.

Swan, K. (2004). Learning online: current research on issues of interface, teaching presence and learner characteristics. In J. Bourne & J. C. Moore (Eds.), *Elements of quality online education, into the mainstream* (pp. 63–79). Needham, MA: Sloan Center for Online Education.

Thurmond, V. A. (2003). *Examination of interaction variables as predictors of students' satisfaction and willingness to enroll in future Web-based courses while controlling for student characteristics.* (Doctoral dissertation), University of Kansas, Retrieved from ProQuest Dissertations Publishing. (UMI No. 3111497)

Thurmond, V. A., & Wambach, K. (2004). Understanding interactions in distance education: A review of the literature. *International Journal of Instructional Technology and Distance Learning, 1*(1), 9–26.

Trentin, G. (1998). Computer conferencing systems as seen by a designer of online courses. *Educational Technology, 38*(3), 36–43.

Vrasidas, C., & McIsaac, M. S. (1999). Factors influencing interaction in an online course. *American Journal of Distance Education, 13*(3), 22–36. doi:10.1080/08923649909527033

Vygotsky, L. S. (1978). *Mind in society: The development of higher psychological processes* (M. Cole, V. John-Steiner, S. Schribner, & E. Souberman, Trans. M. Cole, V. John-Steiner, S. Schribner, & E. Souberman Eds.). Cambridge, MA: Harvard University Press.

Wanstreet, C. E. (2006). Interaction in online learning environments: A review of the literature. *The Quarterly Review of Distance Education, 7*(4), 399–411.

Woods, R. H., & Baker, J. D. (2004). Interaction and immediacy in online learning. *The International Review of Research in Open and Distributed Learning, 5*(2), 13.

Zhang, D. (2005). Interactive multimedia-based e-learning: A study of effectiveness. *The American Journal of Distance Education, 19*(3), 149–162.

Zimmerman, T. D. (2012). Exploring learner to content interaction as a success factor in online courses. *International Review of Research in Open & Distance Learning, 13*(4), 151–165.

3 LMS Log Data Presenting Interaction Traces

Two Types of Interaction Data Recorded by LMSs

To effectively investigate learning and instruction, Chung (2014) clarifies three levels of data useful for understanding learner performance. At the highest macro-level of aggregation is system-level data, the data housed in a student information system (SIS) (Chung, 2014). These data reflect the indicators which are very important to an institution. For example, in a university, the system-level data include learners' course-taking information, course grades, high school information, and demographic information (Chung, 2014). These kinds of data can help answer questions about system-level issues such as retention rates, graduation rates, and time to degree.

The second level is individual-level data generated by traditional education measurements, such as total score on an achievement test, scores on a learning task, or scores on items in a test (Chung, 2014). Previously, data at this level has been regarded as the finest grain-size used in education. But, in recent years, there have been data at an even finer level of detail in technology-based applications, such as data in LMSs and mobile applications (APPs) (Chung, 2014).

Researchers defined this kind of data as 'transaction-level data', which reflects learners' interaction with a digital system where the interaction may be an end in itself (e.g., the action a learner performs) or a means to an end (e.g., the act of uploading an assignment) (Chung, 2014). These interactions are increasingly becoming data sources about learners' temporal choices on learning tasks and are captured and stored in a log format suitable for analyses of learning and instruction (Chung, 2014).

When concentrating on learner interaction, Chung (2014) also proposed two dimensions: outcome measures and process measures. Outcome measures address whether learners were able to complete the task, while process measures address what learners were doing throughout the task. In the first dimension, performance on the task itself is an index of investigation; this approach for performance assessments in online learning is transformed from traditional face-to-face education. The second approach, process measures, is to derive meaningful measures from learners' interaction with

DOI: 10.4324/b23163-4

the technology-based system as they attempt to accomplish the learning objectives (Chung, 2014).

Similarly, Pinnell and colleagues (2017) pointed out two types of data metrics in education: metrics that record learning outcomes, and metrics that record real-time interaction behaviors in learning processes, which may or may not lead to learning outcomes. Learning outcome metrics include metrics such as human-evaluated or computer-evaluated competency scores, evaluations of achievement based on learning goals, self-reported surveys, interviews, and other metrics, which can be easily recorded or captured in online settings as well as traditional instruction settings. Process metrics record real-time interaction behaviors including fine-grained learner behaviors in LMSs with frequency, time, and duration (Pinnell, Paulmani, & Kumar, 2017).

Based on the discussions of previous researchers, in this study, we clarify educational data into two types: a static outcome dimension and a dynamic process dimension. The first type of data includes the system-level data, the individual-level data, and the outcome measures data proposed by Chung (2014) as well as the learning outcome metrics proposed by Pinnell and colleagues (2017). This kind of data records static outcomes of learning and learners' demographic information. The second type of data includes transaction-level data and the process-measures data proposed by Chung (2014) and the learning process metrics proposed by Pinnell and colleagues (2017), which are related to the dynamic process of learning and instruction. As the foundation of educational big data, the database in LMSs not only maintains the demographic information of learners and the contents they get, but also serves to track and structure all the interaction events in the learning and instruction processes (Talavera & Gaudioso, 2004). Such functions are supported by various tools and techniques.

Various tools are defined for carrying out different course projects supporting learners to interact with content, instructor, and peers to conduct meaningful learning (Fernández, Peralta, Benítez, & Herrera, 2014). Take Moodle, a broadly used LMS by online institutions, as an example, Moodle has a flexible array of module activities to create (Romero, Ventura, & García, 2008): five types of static course material (a text page, a web page, a link to anything on the Web, a view into one of the course's directories, and a label that displays any text or image), six types of interactive course material (assignments, choice, journal, lesson, quiz, and survey), and five kinds of activities where learners interact with instructors and each other (chat, forum, glossary, wiki, and workshop). Further, the techniques that support LMSs include content creation and delivery solutions, synchronous and asynchronous communications, and multimedia streaming, capture, and playback systems, all of which provide great infrastructure support for online learning (Brooks, Greer, & Gutwin, 2014). Therefore, the interaction behaviors recorded by log data are various, such as: reading texts, using study guides, watching instructional videos, interacting with multimedia, participating in simulations, searching for information, completing assignments, working on projects, and interacting through the telephone, videoconferencing, chats, e-mail, and discussion boards (Abrami, Bernard, Bures, Borokhovski, & Tamim, 2011).

In general, the difference between interaction activities in LMSs and those activities in traditional instruction settings is that online interactions can be tracked by time sequences through the whole learning process, and LMSs offer various filters depending on parameters such as participants, date, time, and type of activity (Pardo, 2014), which automatically record interaction events with complete details that can not be effectively collected in traditional settings, such as who, when, where, what, and how (Pinnell et al., 2017). Such fine-grained data serve to detect patterns that are tightly coupled with the structure and topic of the activities in online learning, which shows the great potential to clarify the complexity of interaction behavior and improve online learning (Pardo, 2014).

Chung (2014) insisted that the more the dynamic process measures target learners' behavior directly relevant to achieving the outcome, the higher the measures' diagnostic value and their potential to predict the outcomes (Chung, 2014). Therefore, we need to clarify the particular characteristics of dynamic process data and employ effective methods to leverage them.

Temporal and Sequential Characteristics of Interaction Events

In traditional psychology, learning is regarded as a basically unobservable process, taking place in the human brain, an invisible process observed only indirectly by measuring learning outcomes (Reimann, 2009). However, more and more researchers emphasize that learning is not only an outcome but also a dynamic process full of interaction events (Koschmann, 2001; Molenaar, 2014; Reimann, 2009; Stahl, 2010), which is substantially different from the psychological notion of learning. Besides, Reimann (2009) pointed that for both views of learning, the sociocultural as well as the individual-cognitive, the nature of learning process remains temporal and sequential: learning unfolds sequentially over time (Gokhale, 1995; Greene & Azevedo, 2010; Reimann, 2009; Vygotsky, 1978; Zheng, Xing, & Zhu, 2019).

A temporal and sequential conceptualization emphasizes that every interaction event is identified with the specific time and sequence characteristics (Molenaar, 2014). Time comes into present quantitative terms of the interaction event such as durations, rates of change; while sequence also matters because human learning, both self-learning and collaborative learning, is inherently cumulative, how the sequences in the learning process are encountered affects how and what humans learn (Reimann, 2009; Ritter, Nerb, Lehtinen, & O'Shea, 2007).

This conceptual change indicates that traditional measurement, self-report data, has little relation with the dynamic learner behavior during learning (Molenaar, 2014; Veenman, 2011). When interaction and learning are distributed over multiple sessions or contexts, it is difficult to establish the internal validity of our studies (Chung, 2014; Molenaar, 2014; Reimann, 2009). For example, in a long-term process, noncontrolled factors will come into play with a higher probability than is the case for short-term learning, and interaction events become more frequent, which results in qualitative changes in learning (Reimann, 2009). Small differences can have large effects. Both the nature of the data, as well as the nature of the underlying processes, make it impossible to employ traditional methods to collect massive and precise interaction data in real-time (Pistilli, Willis III, & Campbell, 2014; Reimann, 2009; You, 2016). Therefore, this limitation of collecting, organizing, analyzing, and presenting data with traditional measurements leads to strong doubt that self-reported data, such as survey, questionnaire, interview, can properly represent actual learning behaviors in online settings (Guo, 2010; Pistilli et al., 2014; You, 2016).

In addition, traditional statistical methods have relatively limited interpretative power and latency validity in analyzing dynamic process data (Behrens & DiCerbo, 2014; Daniel, 2017). In the past 100 years, the most prominent statistical frameworks centered primarily around the problem of inferring population parameters from small samples (Behrens & DiCerbo, 2014). The classical research practices from these frameworks include 1) linear research steps, 2) a restricted number of possible research designs, and 3) a limited number of research strategies (Cohen, Manion, & Morrison, 2011; Creswell, 2008; Gibson & Ifenthaler, 2017). Null hypothesis significance testing (NHST) is the most common strategy in statistical quantitative analysis. Variables are attributes of fixed entities defined by measurement (e.g., with a scale) or by a coding schema and a counting procedure (Reimann, 2009). Dependent variables and independent variables are the most common terms in NHST analyses. The logic of NHST is based on the question of whether there is a significant effect or not between variables, and whether to support or discredit a priori speculations about some aspect of a population based on a small size of sample (Gibson & Ifenthaler, 2017). Therefore, some researchers name this kind of analysis as the variable-based approach which focuses on the analysis of variance between independent and dependent variable(s) (Molenaar, 2014; Reimann, 2009).

However, temporal and sequential analysis of interaction events is innate to our intuitive understanding of learning, and the conceptualization of this understanding entails a deviation from the NHST research paradigm. This is because it is hard for this NHST approach to answer the questions such as in what ways data are related, within what structures, and with what specific predictable boundaries as well as changing sequences and sets of relationships (Gibson & Ifenthaler, 2017).

Molenaar (2014) emphasized and took the research of Kuvalja and colleagues (2014) as an example to illustrate that data measurement and research methods should match with each other. By employing three different methods, Kuvalja and colleagues (2014) compared the patterns of self-directed speech use during a planning task in typically developing children and matched peers with specific language impairment. The results from the t-pattern analysis revealed that qualitative differences between these two groups in their use of self-directed speech, but the same results were not detected by the other two methods (frequency analysis and lag sequential analysis) (Kuvalja et al., 2014; Magnusson, 2000; Molenaar, 2014). This example indicates that without proper approaches to analyze dynamic process data, existing differences between groups of learners cannot be effectively detected (Molenaar, 2014).

The discussions above point towards the conclusion that traditional measurement and research methods cannot mine the temporal and sequential information embedded in the interaction data tracked by LMSs. It reduces the explanatory power of the analysis and limits the validity of the research conclusions (Molenaar, 2014). Therefore, advances in how such temporal and sequential data are conceptualized and how to employ effective techniques to discover structure, relationships, and sequential patterns from them are the innovative trends in the analysis of online learning.

References

Abrami, P. C., Bernard, R. M., Bures, E. M., Borokhovski, E., & Tamim, R. M. (2011). Interaction in distance education and online learning: Using evidence and theory to improve practice. *Journal of Computing in Higher Education, 23*(2-3), 82–103.

Behrens, J. T., & DiCerbo, K. E. (2014). Harnessing the currents of the digital ocean. In J. A. Larusson & B. White (Eds.), *Learning analytics: From research to practice* (pp. 39–60). New York, NY: Springer Science+Business Media.

Brooks, C., Greer, J., & Gutwin, C. (2014). The data-assisted approach to building intelligent technology-enhanced learning environments. In J. A. Larusson & B. White (Eds.), *Learning analytics: From research to practice* (pp. 123–156). New York, NY: Springer Science+Business Media.

Chung, G. (2014). Toward the relational management of educational measurement data. Retrieved from https://www.ets.org/Media/Research/pdf/chung_toward_relational_management_educational_measurement.pdf

Cohen, L., Manion, L., & Morrison, K. (2011). *Research methods in education* (7th ed.). New York: Routledge.

Creswell, J. W. (2008). *Educational research: Planning, conducting, and evaluating quantitative and qualitative research*. Upper Saddle River, NJ: Pearson.

Daniel, B. K. (2017). Big data in higher education: The big picture. In B. K. Daniel (Ed.), *Big data and learning analytics in higher education* (pp. 19–28). Switzerland: Springer International Publishing.

Fernández, A., Peralta, D., Benítez, J. M., & Herrera, F. (2014). E-learning and educational data mining in cloud computing: an overview. *International Journal of Learning Technology, 9*(1), 25–52.

Gibson, D., & Ifenthaler, D. (2017). Preparing the next generation of education researchers for big data in higher education. In B. K. Daniel (Ed.), *Big data and learning analytics in higher education* (pp. 29–42). Switzerland: Springer International Publishing.

Gokhale, A. A. (1995). Collaborative learning and critical thinking. *Journal of Technology Education 7*, 22–30.

Greene, J. A., & Azevedo, R. (2010). The measurement of learners' self-regulated cognitive and metacognitive processes while using computer-based learning environments. *Educational Psychologist, 45*(4), 203–209.

Guo, W. W. (2010). Incorporating statistical and neural network approaches for student course satisfaction analysis and prediction. *Expert Systems with Applications, 37*(4), 3358–3365.

Koschmann, T. D. (2001). *Revising the paradigms of instructional technology*. Paper presented at the 8th Annual Conference of the Australasian Society for Computers in Learning in Tertiary Education (ASCILITE).

Kuvalja, M., Kuvalja, M., Verma, M., Verma, M., Whitebread, D., & Whitebread, D. (2014). Patterns of co-occurring non-verbal behaviour and self-directed speech; a comparison of three methodological approaches. *Metacognition and Learning, 9*(2), 87–111. doi: 10.1007/s11409-013-9106-7

Magnusson, M. (2000). Discovering hidden time patterns in behavior: T-patterns and their detection. *Behavior Research Methods, Instruments, and Computers, 32*(1), 93–110.

Molenaar, I. (2014). Advances in temporal analysis in learning and instruction. *Frontline Learning Research, 2*(4), 15–24.

Pardo, A. (2014). Designing Learning Analytics experiences. In J. A. Larusson & B. White (Eds.), *Learning analytics: From research to practice* (pp. 15–38). New York, NY: Springer Science+Business Media.

Pinnell, C., Paulmani, G., & Kumar, V. (2017). Curricular and learning analytics: A big data perspective. In B. K. Daniel (Ed.), *Big data and learning analytics in higher education* (pp. 125–145). Switzerland: Springer International Publishing.

Pistilli, M. D., Willis III, J. E., & Campbell, J. P. (2014). Analytics through an institutional lens: Definition, theory, design, and impact. In J. A. Larusson & B. White (Eds.), *Learning analytics: From research to practice* (pp. 79–102). New York, NY: Springer Science+Business Media.

Reimann, P. (2009). Time is precious: Variable- and event-centred approaches to process analysis in CSCL research. *International Journal of Computer-Supported Collaborative Learning, 4*(3), 239–257. doi:10.1007/s11412-009-9070-z

Ritter, F. E., Nerb, J., Lehtinen, E., & O'Shea, T. M. (2007). *In order to learn: How the sequences of topics influences learning*. Oxford: Oxford University Press.

Romero, C., Ventura, S., & García, E. (2008). Data mining in course management systems: Moodle case study and tutorial. *Computers & Education, 51*(1), 368–384.

Stahl, G. (2010). Group cognition: Computer support for building collaborative knowledge. *Journal of the Association for Information Science & Technology, 59*(9), 1531–1531.

Talavera, L., & Gaudioso, E. (2004, August). *Mining student data to characterize similar behavior groups in unstructured collaboration spaces*. Paper presented at the Workshop on Artificial Intelligence in CSCL, the 16th European Conference on Artificial Intelligence (ECAI 2004), Valencia, Spain.

Veenman, M. V. J. (2011). Learning to self-monitor and self-regulate. In R. Mayer & P. Alexander (Eds.), *Handbook of research on learning and instruction* (pp. 197–218). New York: Routledge.

Vygotsky, L. S. (1978). *Mind in society: The development of higher psychological processes* (M. Cole, V. John-Steiner, S. Schribner, & E. Souberman, Trans. M. Cole, V. John-Steiner, S. Schribner, & E. Souberman Eds.). Cambridge, MA: Harvard University Press.

You, J. W. (2016). Identifying significant indicators using LMS data to predict course achievement in online learning. *Internet and Higher Education, 29*, 23–30.

Zheng, J., Xing, W., & Zhu, G. (2019). Examining sequential patterns of self- and socially shared regulation of STEM learning in a CSCL environment. *Computers & Education, 136*, 34–48. doi: 10.1016/j.compedu.2019.03.005

4 Interaction Research with Learning Analytics

Learning Analytics Methodology

Advances in the accuracy of data measurements deepen the understanding of the phenomena being observed. Take the innovation of the microscope as an example: as the resolving power of the instrument has increased, so have significant advances in a scientific investigation (Chung, 2014; Laesecke, 2002). We are now approaching a similar potential in the measurement of learners' learning processes using technology-based devices such as LMSs and APPs. Data from these devices record fine-grained information about what learners do as well as capture the context surrounding the behavior, which allows decoding learning processes and states that were previously invisible. The analysis of interaction events is driven by the realization that, without careful attention to temporal and sequential characteristics, we are reducing the significance of our research and are unable to explain important aspects of learning and instruction. Fortunately, as a new methodology in educational research, learning analytics focuses on the development of methods for analyzing and detecting patterns within data collected from educational settings and leverages those methods to support the learning experience (Larusson & White, 2014).

A pivotal difference to the variable-centered NHST method is that learning analytics does not start by framing the constructs in terms of variables as fixed entities with varying attributes (Poole, van de Ven, Dooley, & Holmes, 2000; Reimann, 2009). Learning analytics is an event-based approach, which looks at the development and change of events and analyzes the dynamic relations between them over a long time (Baker & Inventado, 2016; Gibson & Ifenthaler, 2017; Larusson & White, 2014; Molenaar, 2014). Consistency and change of the patterns in learning behaviors can be investigated by specifying these temporal and sequential characteristics (Molenaar, 2014; Schmitz, 2006). Thus, it ameliorates the risks of confirmation bias that are inherent in traditional statistics; and it is possible to discover structural patterns that might be missed in traditional statistics with only a single theoretical construct, pre-test and post-test data points, or pre-selected hypothesis being tested (Ocumpaugh, Baker, Gowda, Heffernan, & Heffernan, 2014).

DOI: 10.4324/b23163-5

The methods of learning analytics are divided into prediction modeling, relationship mining, structure discovery, distillation of data for human judgment, and discovery with models (Baker & Inventado, 2016).

Prediction modeling is to develop a model to infer a single aspect of the data (the predicted variable) from some combination of other aspects of the data (predictor variables). In learning analytics, classification and regression are the most common types of prediction models as well as latent knowledge estimation (Baker & Inventado, 2016).

Relationship mining is to discover relationships between variables in a dataset with another large number of variables. This may take the form of attempting to find variable(s) most strongly associated with a single variable of particular interest, or may take the form of attempting to discover which relationships between any two variables are strongest (Baker & Inventado, 2016). Baker and Siemens (2014) identified four common relationship mining types in learning analytics: correlation mining, association rule mining, sequential pattern mining, and causal data mining (Baker & Siemens, 2014).

Structure discovery attempts to use algorithms to find structure in the data without a priori idea of what should be found (Baker & Inventado, 2016). Common approaches to structure discovery in learning analytics include clustering, factor analysis, social network analysis, and domain structure discovery (Baker & Siemens, 2014).

Data distilled for human judgment in learning analytics serve two key purposes: identification and classification (Baker & Inventado, 2016). The methods of learning analytics are information visualization methods (Baker & Siemens, 2014). For example, a learning curve displays the number of opportunities to practice a skill on the X-axis, and displays performance (such as percent correct or time taken to respond) on the Y-axis (Baker, 2010); instructors can incorporate those data quickly into instructional strategies.

In *discovery with models*, a model of a phenomenon is developed via prediction, clustering, or in some cases knowledge engineering; this model is then used as a component in a second analysis or model, for example in Prediction or Relationship mining (Baker & Siemens, 2014). In the case of learning analytics, one common use is when an initial model's predictions (which represent predicted variables in the original model) become predictor variables in a new prediction model (Baker & Inventado, 2016).

Based on the general review of the approaches above, we can see learning analytics is a specific methodology to answer the questions deriving from LMSs log data, such as those ones mentioned above: what ways data are related within structures, and with what specific predictable bounded as well as changing sequences and sets of relationships (Gibson & Ifenthaler, 2017).

Over the past 10 years, there has been a continued increase in observing learning behavior and analyzing the data generated by learners' interaction with digital devices in LMSs. The techniques of learning analytics help target instructional and curricular resources to facilitate learners to achieve specific learning goals. The goal of learning analytics is to enable instructors and institutions to tailor the educational experiences of individual learners in near real time.

Interaction Research with Data from Discourse, Video, and Brainwave

As evidenced in the literature, a lot of research on the temporality and sequence analysis has investigated the distribution patterns of discourse, video data, and brainwave data. In addition, most of the studies have been carried out in collaborative learning environments.

Chiu and Khoo (2005) collected 3,104 speaker turns from 80 middle school learners in 20 collaborative groups (Chiu & Khoo, 2005). These learners worked on an algebra word problem in groups of four learners each. Each group was videotaped for one learning session, and distinct time periods existed within each session. During each session, researchers observed a stream of sequential behavior, and then this stream of sequential behavior was parsed into discrete behaviors. The hypothesis of their study was that the general class of phenomena of current events was being affected by recent past events (and also by non-time-dependent characteristics). Two research assistants coded each speaker turn for the following: correctness, speaker's mathematics status, and evaluation of the previous speaker. Researchers tested the hypothesis and investigated the sequential processes of these time-series data through four different methods: conditional probabilities, sequential analysis, Logit, and dynamic multilevel analysis (DMA). Particularly, they illustrated that except for DMA, all the other three methods failed to address heterogeneity across time or across groups (Chiu & Khoo, 2005).

To gain an in-depth understanding of the features and limitations of the digital guide systems in a museum-learning context, Sung and colleagues (2010) conducted sequential analysis and frequency analysis to identify features determining different behavioral interaction patterns (Sung, Hou, Liu, & Chang, 2010). The learning behaviors recorded on video of 65 elementary-school learners in three groups with different learning strategies: a mobile guide with problem-solving strategy, an audio-visual mobile guide, and a paper-based learning-sheet guide. Researchers first coded the behaviors in the video, and then analyzed learning-related discussion content. Behavioral interaction patterns were determined by comparing the features and limitations of the different types of guides. They found that the learners in the problem-solving mobile guide group showed a higher level of two-way interactions with their peers and the exhibits, as well as more learning-related discussions (Sung et al., 2010). Therefore, relevant design suggestions for teachers, researchers, and guide-systems developers were provided that can better guide learners in interacting with peers and exhibitions.

Chu and colleagues (2016) proposed a novel data mining method to detect and analyze frequent learning discussion patterns in MOOCs forums. The data were collected from the content of the 400 questions and answers from the forum for the course 'Programming for Everybody (Getting started with Python)'; the learning interaction discussion was constructed as a tree-structured pattern. LIP-Miner algorithm was designed to analyze learners' and instructors' interactions to find frequent interaction patterns. Finally, the results proved that the proposed algorithm can find interesting learning interaction patterns in MOOCs forums (Chu, Wang, & Kuo, 2016).

To examine how temporal sequences of regulated learning events emerge during different stages of collaborative learning, Malmberg and colleagues (2017) conducted a temporal and sequential analysis based on 22 hours of video data during a two-month didactics course. The participants were teacher education learners who collaborated in three-member groups. The video data were collected to follow how sequences of regulated learning events, along with task execution, emerged within the six groups as their collaboration advanced. Qualitative content analysis and lag sequential analysis were used to analyze the data. The results showed that the groups engaged mostly in co-regulated planning and monitoring, and metacognitive monitoring played a facilitative role in the progress of task execution (Malmberg, Järvelä, & Järvenoja, 2017). Also, task execution provided grounding for socially shared planning and regulation to occur (Malmberg et al., 2017).

Similarly, to emphasize that collaborative learning is actualized through evolving dialogues, Chen and colleagues (2017) uncovered sequential patterns that distinguish 'productive' threads of knowledge-building discourse. The database was based on learners' discourse from Grade 1 to 6, which was first coded for the posts' contribution types and discussion threads' productivity. Two different techniques, Lag Sequential Analysis (LSA) and Frequent Sequence Mining (FSM), were employed to identify the sequential patterns which aim to distinguish productive threads. LSA indicated that threads that were characterized by mere opinion-giving did not achieve much progress, while threads having more transitions among questioning, obtaining information, working with information, and theorizing was more productive. The results of FSM uncovered productive threads distinguishing frequent sequences involving sustained theorizing, integrated use of evidence, and problematization of proposed theories (Chen, Resendes, Chai, & Hong, 2017).

In 2019, Zheng and colleagues examined sequences of both self- and socially shared activities in the online chats and logs of learners, and how the sequences influenced group performance (Zheng, Xing, & Zhu, 2019). The data were from 156 learners completing a STEM task in a computer-supported collaborative learning (CSCL) environment in high school and college. They were randomly assigned to groups of three and asked to solve four tasks of increasing complexity in a virtual learning environment designed to teach learners about electronics. The results revealed that successful groups demonstrated more frequent and more diverse regulatory activities than the less successful ones. Also, the successful groups were most likely to start with self-executing and end with socially shared monitoring, while the less successful group was most likely to start with executing and end with self-executing. In addition, the timing of socially shared monitoring influences the success of collaborative learning (Zheng et al., 2019).

Interaction Research with Log Data

Another line of research has focused on revealing a bigger picture of sequential patterns by investigating log files that learners left in LMSs.

Soller and Lesgold (2007) employed HMMs to model the process of a collaborative learning process to have a fine-grained sequential analysis of group activity and collaboration (Soller & Lesgold, 2007). They presented the collaborative learning process from multiple perspectives, which focus on the behaviors driving explanation, critiques, sharing, and motivation. The desired goal was to better understand the interaction and to provide advice or support to learners. They discussed five different computational approaches for modeling collaborative learning: Finite State Machines, Rule Learners, Decision Trees, Plan Recognition, and Hidden Markov Models; and particularly illustrated the Hidden Markov modeling approach in detail. The result showed that the Hidden Markov model performs significantly better than statistical analysis in recognizing the knowledge sharer and the knowledge recipients when learners exchange new knowledge during learning activities.

Nesbit and colleagues (2007) collected log files generated by 103 university learners in their self-regulated learning using gStudy. gStudy is a software application developed by the researchers, which supports learners to create and link notes, highlight and label text and images, construct glossaries and concept maps, exchange information objects through a chat interface, and perform other operations on multimedia content. With the support of gStudy, researchers used log parsing and data mining methods to identify coherent learning actions from the complex series of low-level events and detect sequential patterns common to a group of participants that may be interspersed with unrelated actions (Nesbit, Zhou, Xu, & Winne, 2007).

Perera and colleagues (2009) focused on collaborative learning and employed clustering and sequential pattern mining to investigate interaction trace data of online collaborative learning. There were 43 learners in seven groups who participated in the collaborative teamwork in an online project management system called TRAC; the interaction data were recorded from mirroring and feedback tools in TRAC. The researchers aimed to exploit these data to support mirroring by presenting useful high-level views of information about the group, and the desired patterns characterizing the behavior of strong groups. The goal was to enable the groups and their facilitators to see relevant aspects of the group's operation and provide feedback if these were more likely to be associated with positive or negative outcomes and where the problems are (Perera, Kay, Koprinska, Yacef, & Zaïane, 2009). Researchers first used k-means clustering to cluster similar teams and similar learners and then employed a modified version of the Generalized Sequential Pattern mining algorithm to identify the important interaction patterns associated with success. They extracted patterns from three sessions: group and author session, task sequence, and resource session. For each set of results, they sorted the patterns first on support, then on length, and compared the results across groups; finally, they identified which patterns were most frequent in certain groups and least frequent in other groups. Patterns distinguishing the stronger groups from the weaker groups were extracted, which help researchers gain insights into success factors, such as leadership and group interaction and providing promising indications. In addition, patterns indicating good individual practices were also identified. The results suggested the effectiveness of identifying effective and poor practices early, advising groups at the start of learning, and providing remediation in time. In their study, all groups improved their achievements by observation and emulation of the interaction patterns from stronger groups (Perera et al., 2009).

Jeong and colleagues (2010) conducted an exploratory sequence analysis by applying the Hidden Markov model approach to investigate learners' learning behaviors and the evolution of interaction activity of different learner groups in an asynchronous online learning environment. The environment was derived from the STAR Legacy Cycle which is a software shell designed to organize learning activities as an inquiry cycle; the learners of this system are adult professionals, who took this course as a degree requirement or for professional certification. Researchers hypothesized that learners in different performance groups will employ different

Learning behavior patterns (and likely, different strategies); further, learners' behavior patterns will evolve as they study different course content (Jeong, Biswas, Johnson, & Howard, 2010). Therefore, they decided to focus on examining the differences in behaviors between the high and the low performers on the system to provide insights on how learning behaviors relate to performance (Jeong et al., 2010). The learners were divided into high performers and low performers based on the posttest scores. The learning process based on the STAR Legacy Cycle was represented in modules: Challenge (C), presenting problem descriptions; Initial Thoughts (T), learners' initial thoughts providing; Resources (R), learning about the problem; Self-Assessment (A), answering assessment questions; Wrap-up (W), reviewing and concluding. The analysis focused on the six types of transition behaviors learners made among the five modules: *linear* (L), *jumping* (J), *retrying* (R), *searching* (S), *transitioning* (T), and *backtracking* (B). After preprocessing the data, activity sequences were arranged in the format consisting of a series of transition-context pairs such as AR-Linear, RR-Linear, RR-Retrying, and so on. A Hidden Markov model approach was employed to investigate the difference between the two performance groups and how the learning behaviors in each group evolved in different course process. The results demonstrated that high-performing learners had more linear learning behaviors and that their behaviors remained consistent across different course processes (Jeong et al., 2010).

Martinez and colleagues (2011) reported a study to analyze frequent sequential patterns of collaborative learning activity around an interactive tabletop named Digital Mysteries. The goal was to discover which frequent sequences of actions differentiate high achieving from low achieving groups. Eighteen elementary school learners took part in the study, forming six groups of three participants; every action of participants on the tabletop was logged and all sessions were video recorded. Six groups of participants generated a total of 12 logged sessions. The raw data were coded as a series of Events, where Event = (Time, Author, Action, Object). The possible actions that can be performed on the data slips are: moving, enlarging to maximum size, resizing to medium size, shrinking, rotating, making unions with other data slips, add data slip to a group, and remove a data slip from a group (Martinez, Yacef, Kay, Kharrufa, & Al-Qaraghuli, 2011). Out of the 12 logged sessions by six groups, five were coded as low achieving groups, five as high achieving groups, and two as average groups. Researchers focused on the 10 sessions that clearly showed evidence of low or high achievement. They explored two pre-processing approaches. The first method went straight into the sequence mining, and the second method compacted similar contiguous actions before applying the sequence mining. After pre-processing the data and conducting sequence mining to determine frequent patterns, researchers employed hierarchical agglomerative clustering technique (Witten & Frank, 1999) to cluster similar frequent patterns determined by sequence mining (Martinez et al., 2011). The results from both of the two methods indicated that learners of high achieving groups tried to interact and externalize their thinking. These students tended to read all the slips to get clues about the mystery and parallel interactions were clearly observed along with engagement in conversations. On the other hand, learners of low achieving groups tended to simply move or rotate the data slips, make unions with other slips, or add slips to a group (Martinez et al., 2011).

Kinnebrew and colleagues (2013) employed a contextualized and differential sequence mining method to assess and compare the interaction behaviors of 40 8th grade learners in online settings. Researchers conducted this exploratory methodology to learning interaction trace data gathered during a middle school class study with online tools called Betty's Brain. They expected learners using Betty's Brain to typically iterate between reading material and teaching Betty by building the causal map, while also checking and reflecting on Betty's and their own understanding of the domain knowledge. To analyze the interaction traces of learners, researchers abstracted and divided interaction actions into five categories: (1) READ, learners read the resources; (2) Editing, actions such as link or concept, and add, remove, or modify; (3) QUER: learners query Betty; (4) EXPL: learners ask Betty to explain her answer to a query; (5) QUIZ: learners have Betty take a quiz. The novel combination of sequence mining techniques developed by the researchers can directly incorporate comparisons between groups when identifying interesting patterns, rather than manually performing comparisons. In addition to sequential pattern mining metrics, researchers employed another frequency calculation based on episode mining to identify and rank differentially frequent patterns. With the support of these sequence analysis techniques, they identified differentially frequent patterns between learners in the high (Hi) performance group and learners in the low (Lo) performance group. The results indicated that the learners in Hi group were more likely to follow a quiz with relevant reading or queries, while the learners in Lo group were more likely to follow a quiz with unrelated reading. Also, the results suggested a differential effort by the Hi group to use monitoring strategies that made more effective use of the quiz results, and these strategies may indicate that the Hi group learners paid more attention to the feedback or were better able to understand and implement the monitoring feedback (Kinnebrew, Loretz, & Biswas, 2013).

Guerra and colleagues (2014) modeled and examined patterns of learner behavior with parameterized exercises using Problem Solving Genome, a compact encapsulation of individual behavior patterns. They started with micro-patterns (genomes) that describe small chunks of repetitive behavior and constructed individual genomes as frequency profiles that show the dominance of each gene in individual behavior (Guerra, Sahebi, Lin, & Brusilovsky, 2014). With the genome, researchers analyzed learner behavior on the group level and identified genes associated with good and bad learning performance. The results revealed that individual patterns can distinguish learners from their peers and change very little with the growth of knowledge over the course (Guerra et al., 2014).

To identify new factors of prediction of academic success, Venant and colleagues (2017) used a sequential pattern mining approach to analyze relations between learners' activities during practical sessions, and their performance at the final assessment test. The data were collected from experimentation conducted with a remote lab dedicated to computer education. Researchers discovered recurrent sequential patterns of actions. These patterns may be evidence which defines learning strategies as indicators of a higher level of abstraction (Venant, Sharma, Vidal, Dillenbourg, & Broisin, 2017). They found that the construction of a complex action step by step, or the reflection before submitting an action, are two strategies applied more often by learners of a higher level of performance than by other learners, which illustrated that some of the strategies are correlated to learners' performance (Venant et al., 2017).

In 2018, Doko and colleagues tried to decode mobile learning processes by coming up with a methodology for performing video learning data history of learner's video watching logs, video segments or time-series data analyzing learners' video watching logs, video segments, or time-series data. They introduced a theoretical method of sequential pattern mining to identify the most important or difficult learning. They also described a model for understanding the most difficult topics. Their method can generate sequences from the collected learning histories, extract important patterns from a set of sequences, and find learners' most difficult/important topics from the extracted patterns. Also, they recommended implementing this method to use in mobile phones in the future (Doko, Abazi Bexheti, Hamiti, & Prevalla, 2018).

Interaction Research with Log Data in Particular Topics

Other researchers employed sequential and temporal analysis with log files in particular areas such as learning style, concept mapping process, game-based learning, and recommendation systems.

Graf and colleagues (2010) pointed out that supporting learners by considering their learning styles in the computer-assisted environment has a high potential for making learning easier or increasing learners' performance (Graf, Liu, & Kinshuk, 2010). Therefore, they investigated the patterns of learners' navigation behavior in an online course. Several differences in the learners' behavioral patterns were identified, which indicated that learners with different learning styles used different ways to learn and interact with the course. Similarly, Fatahi and colleagues (2018) realized that identifying sequential behavior patterns can provide useful information for determining the learning style (Fatahi, Shabanali-Fami, & Moradi, 2018). They extracted frequent sequential behavior patterns which can separate learners with different learning styles, and then predicted a learner's learning style during their interaction with an e-learning system. The results showed that learning styles can be predicted with high accuracy.

To help understand learners' learning process, some researchers turned their attention to game-based learning environments to mine sequential behavior patterns. Hou (2012) compiled a log of learners' operations on a large-scale multi-person online educational gaming platform to analyze learners' knowledge construction, peer interaction, and problem-solving processes (Hou, 2012). Later, Hou (2015) investigated behavioral patterns and flow states in game-based learning to understand the patterns of their interactive behavior during learning (Hou, 2015). In 2017, Kang and colleagues conducted a study that uses gameplay data captured as a learner interacts with various tools embedded in a game environment (Kang, Liu, & Qu, 2017). Their study expanded on previous research on learners' cognitive process patterns by incorporating the combination of statistical analysis with sequential pattern mining in an investigation of learning patterns among learners with different expertise.

Inspired by the application of sequential pattern mining techniques in various learning settings, an approach for exploring learner sequential patterns in constructing concept maps was proposed by Chiu and Lin (2012). To validate the proposed method, the concept mapping data from 187 college learners were analyzed by the sequential pattern analysis method. The results revealed that the mapping sequences used by learners that created superior concept maps were similar and had a pattern in which propositions were formed in temporal order from more inclusive to less inclusive (Chiu & Lin, 2012). Similarly, in 2018, Sun and colleagues conducted a sequence analysis exploring the effects of integrated concept maps and classroom polling systems on learners' learning performance, attentional behavior, and brainwaves associated with attention (Sun et al., 2018). The data from 21 college learners were collected through in-class quizzes, attentional behavior analysis, a 20-minute structured interview, and the attention-associated brainwaves. The results showed that the pen and paper concept mapping approach improved the quiz results of learners with lower learning motivation prior to the course, while the votable concept mapping method was effective in stimulating learners' attention during class.

Recommendation system is another application of temporal and sequential analysis. A recommendation could be based on the teacher's intended sequence of navigation or navigation patterns of other successful learners, which is because other learners with similar learning status will have the same experience with these resources (Klašnja-Milićević, Vesin, & Ivanović, 2018). For example, Chen and colleagues (2014) proposed a hybrid recommender system framework based on learners' sequential patterns. After filtering content-related item sets, they applied a sequential pattern mining algorithm to discover items according to common learning sequences; therefore, potentially useful learning items were identified and recommended to guide users in their learning processes (Chen, Niu, Zhao, & Li, 2014).

Discussion

As mentioned above, a number of studies have conducted sequential and temporal mining techniques to extract learners' behavior patterns based on discourse data, video data, log data, as well as the data of brainwaves. These data are from learners in primary schools, high schools, colleges, and MOOCs. The educational environments include collaborative learning, self-regulated learning, game-based learning, or concept mapping activities. Some of the studies illustrated the effectiveness and stability of sequential and temporal analysis in exploring learners' interaction behaviors in learning. Some of them used sequence patterns to distinguish learners with different performances, cognition levels, meta-cognition levels, or learning styles. Some of them applied behavior patterns in developing recommendation systems. These analyses that reveal various interaction patterns about sequential and temporal interactions at the micro-level mainly concentrate on two essential questions: 'What do these relations among interaction patterns mean for learning, and which patterns should we encourage in learning and instruction?'

However, most of these efforts were carried out under experimental or quasi-experimental conditions with few participants and a short time span. None of them has tried to extract action patterns based on interaction behaviors in daily massive online courses that support massive learners with regular learning behaviors through an entire semester in online settings. That is because the massive online learners, long-term learning process, non-experimental environment, and huge data files are big challenges for researchers to analyze fine-grained learning action at the micro-level.

Therefore, this study aims to find sequential patterns that can distinguish learners based on their interaction actions in a very particular environment ignored by most researchers: MPOCs settings.

References

Abrami, P. C., Bernard, R. M., Bures, E. M., Borokhovski, E., & Tamim, R. M. (2011). Interaction in distance education and online learning: Using evidence and theory to improve practice. *Journal of Computing in Higher Education, 23*(2-3), 82–103.

Allen, I. E., & Seaman, J. (2010). Class differences: Online education in the United States, 2010. *Sloan Consortium (NJ1)*, 30.

Allen, I. E., & Seaman, J. (2016). Online report card: Tracking online education in the United States. *Babson Survey Research Group.*

Allen, M., Bourhis, J., Burrell, N., & Mabry, E. (2002). Comparing student satisfaction with distance education to traditional classrooms in higher education: A meta-analysis. *The American Journal of Distance Education, 16*(2), 83–97.

Anderson, T. (2003). Getting the mix right again: An updated and theoretical rationale for interaction. *International Review of Research in Open & Distance Learning, 4*(2), 65-65.

Antonenko, P. D., Toy, S., & Niederhauser, D. S. (2012). Using cluster analysis for data mining in educational technology research. *Educational Technology Research and Development, 60*(3), 383–398.

Atack, L., & Rankin, J. (2002). A descriptive study of registered nurses' experiences with web-based learning. *Journal of Advanced Nursing, 40*, 457–465.

Bahl, L., Brown, P. F., De Souza, P. V., & Mercer, R. L. (1986). Maximum mutual information estimation of hidden Markov model parameters for speech recognition. *Proceedings of the IEEE-IECEJ-AS International Conference on Acoustics, Speech, and Signal Processing, 1*, 49–52.

Baker, R. (2010). Data mining for education. In B. McGaw, P. Peterson, & E. Baker (Eds.), *International encyclopedia of education* (3rd ed., pp. 112–118). Oxford, UK: Elsevier.

Baker, R., & Inventado, P. S. (2016). Educational data mining and learning analytics: Potentials and possibilities for online education. In G. Veletsianos (Ed.), *Emergence and innovation in digital learning: Foundations and applications* (pp. 83–98). Edmonton, AB, Canada: Athabasca University Press.

Baker, R., & Siemens, G. (2014). Educational data mining and Learning Analytics. In K. Sawyer (Ed.), *Cambridge handbook of the learning sciences* (2nd ed., pp. 253–274). New York, NY: Cambridge University Press.

Barkley, E. F., Cross, K. P., & Major, C. H. (2014). *Collaborative learning techniques: A handbook for college faculty*. San Francisico, CA: John Wiley & Sons.

Bates, A. W. (1995). *Technology, open Learning and distance education*. New York, NY: Routledge.

Baum, L. E., Petrie, T., Soules, G., & Weiss, N. (1970). A maximization technique occurring in the statistical analysis of probabilistic functions of Markov chains. *Annals of Mathematical Statistics*, *41*(1), 164–171.

Behrens, J. T., & DiCerbo, K. E. (2014). Harnessing the currents of the digital ocean. In J. A. Larusson & B. White (Eds.), *Learning Analytics: From research to practice* (pp. 39–60). New York, NY: Springer Science+Business Media.

Ben-Yishai, A., & Burshtein, D. (2004). A discriminative training algorithm for hidden Markov models. *IEEE Transactions on Speech and Audio Processing 12*(3), 204–217. doi:10.1109/TSA.2003.822639

Bernard, R. M., Abrami, P. C., Lou, Y., Borokhovski, E., Wade, A., Wozney, L., … Huang, B. (2004). How does distance education compare with classroom instruction? A meta-analysis of the empirical literature. *Review of educational research*, *74*(3), 379–439.

Billings, D. M., Connors, H. R., & Skiba, D. J. (2001). Benchmarking best practices in web-based nursing courses. *Advances in Nursing Science*, *23*(3), 41–52.

Bomatpalli, T. (2014). Learning Analytics and Big Data in higher education. *International Journal of Engineering Research & Technology*, *3*(1), 3377–3383.

Bouhnik, D., & Marcus, T. (2006). Interaction in distance-learning courses. *Journal of the American Society for Information Science and Technology*, *57*(3), 299–305.

Brooks, C., Greer, J., & Gutwin, C. (2014). The data-assisted approach to building intelligent technology-enhanced learning environments. In J. A. Larusson & B. White (Eds.), *Learning Analytics: From research to practice* (pp. 123–156). New York, NY: Springer Science+Business Media.

Browning, J. B. (1999). *Analysis of concepts and skills acquisition differences between Web-delivered and classroom-delivered undergraduate instructional technology courses*. (Doctoral dissertation), Retrieved from ProQuest Dissertations Publishing. (UMI No. 9938354)

Cavanaugh, C. S. (2001). The effectiveness of interactive distance education technologies in K-12 learning: A meta-analysis. *International Journal of Educational Telecommunications*, *7*(1), 73.

Cerezo, R., Sánchez-Santillán, M., Paule-Ruiz, M. P., & Núñez, J. C. (2016). Students' LMS interaction patterns and their relationship with achievement: A case study in higher education. *Computers & Education*, *96*, 42–54.

Chan, J., Hew, K. F., & Cheung, W. S. (2009). Asynchronous online discussion thread development: examining growth patterns and peer-facilitation techniques. *Journal of Computer Assisted Learning*, *25*(5), 438–452.

Chatti, M. A., Muslim, A., & Schroeder, U. (2017). Toward an open Learning Analytics ecosystem. In B. K. Daniel (Ed.), *Big Data and Learning Analytics in higher education* (pp. 195–219). Switzerland: Springer International Publishing.

Chen, B., Resendes, M., Chai, C. S., & Hong, H.-Y. (2017). Two tales of time: Uncovering the significance of sequential patterns among contribution types in knowledge-building discourse. *Interactive Learning Environments*, *25*(2), 162–175. doi:10.1080/10494820.2016.1276081

Chen, L. (2004). An investigation into" Interactivity" and the related concepts. *China Distance Education*, *3*, 12–19.

Chen, W., Niu, Z., Zhao, X., & Li, Y. (2014). A hybrid recommendation algorithm adapted in e-learning environments. *World Wide Web*, *17*(2), 271–284. doi:10.1007/s11280-012-0187-z

Chiu, C., & Lin, C. (2012). Sequential pattern analysis: Method and application in exploring how students develop concept maps. *The Turkish Online Journal of Educational Technology*, *11*(1), 145–153.

Chiu, M., & Khoo, L. (2005). A new method for analyzing sequential processes: Dynamic multi-level analysis. *Small Group Research*, *36*, 600–631. doi:10.1177/1046496405279309

Chu, K. C., Wang, C. S., & Kuo, J. H. (2016). *Mining of learning interaction patterns in MOOCs forums*. Paper presented at the 17th international conference on information reuse and integration (IRI), Pittsburgh, PA, USA.

Chung, G. (2014). Toward the relational management of educational measurement data. Retrieved from https://www.ets.org/Media/Research/pdf/chung_toward_relational_management_educational_measurement.pdf

Clark, R. C., & Mayer, R. E. (2016). *E-Learning and the science of instruction*. Hobaken, NJ: John Wiley & Sons, Inc.

Cohen, L., Manion, L., & Morrison, K. (2011). *Research Methods in Education* (7th ed.). New York: Routledge.

Compton-Lilly, C. (2013). Temporal discourse analysis. In T. Holbrook, P. Albers, & A. F. Routledge (Eds.), *New Methods on Literacy Research* (pp. 40–55). London, UK: Routledge.

Creswell, J. W. (2008). *Educational research: Planning, conducting, and evaluating quantitative and qualitative research*. Upper Saddel River, NJ: Pearson.

Daley, B. J., Watkins, K., Williams, S. W., Courtenay, B., Davis, M., & Dymock, D. (2001). Exploring learning in a technology-enhanced environment. *Journal of Educational Technology & Society*, *4*(3), 126–138.

Daniel, B. K. (2017). Big Data in higher education: The big picture. In B. K. Daniel (Ed.), *Big Data and Learning Analytics in higher education* (pp. 19–28). Switzerland: Springer International Publishing.

Dawson, S. P., McWilliam, E., & Tan, J. P.-L. (2008). Teaching smarter: How mining ICT data can inform and improve learning and teaching practice. http://www.ascilite.org.au/conferences/melbourne08/procs/dawson.pdf

de Freitas, S. I., Morgan, J., & Gibson, D. (2015). Will MOOCs transform learning and teaching in higher education? Engagement and course retention in online learning provision. *British Journal of Educational Technology*, *46*(3), 455–471.

Dennen, V. P., Aubteen Darabi, A., & Smith, L. J. (2007). Instructor–learner interaction in online courses: The relative perceived importance of particular instructor actions on performance and satisfaction. *Distance Education*, *28*(1), 65–79.

Dillenbourg, P. (1999). What do you mean by collaborative learning? In P. Dillenbourg (Ed.), *Collaborative learning: Cognitive and computational approaches* (pp. 1–19). Amsterdam: Elsevier Science.

Doko, E., Abazi Bexheti, L., Hamiti, M., & Prevalla, B. (2018). Sequential pattern mining model to identify the most important or difficult learning topics via mobile technologies. *International Journal of Interactive Mobile Technologies (iJIM)*, *12*, 109–122. doi:10.3991/ijim.v12i4.9223

Dolence, M. G., & Norris, D. M. (1995). *Transforming higher education: a vision for learning in the 21st century*. Ann Arbor, MI: Society for College and University Planning.

Dringus, L. P. (2012). Learning analytics considered harmful. *Journal of Asynchronous Learning Networks, 16*(3), 87–100.

Fatahi, S., Shabanali-Fami, F., & Moradi, H. (2018). An empirical study of using sequential behavior pattern mining approach to predict learning styles. *Education and Information Technologies, 23*(4), 1427–1445. doi:10.1007/s10639-017-9667-1

Fernández, A., Peralta, D., Benítez, J. M., & Herrera, F. (2014). E-learning and educational data mining in cloud computing: an overview. *International Journal of Learning Technology, 9*(1), 25–52.

Fredericksen, E., Pickett, A., Shea, P., Pelz, W., & Swan, K. (2000). Student satisfaction and perceived learning with online courses-principles and examples from the SUNY learning network. *Journal of Asynchronous Learning Networks, 4*(2), 7–41.

García, E., Romero, C., Ventura, S., & Calders, T. (2007). *Drawbacks and solutions of applying association rule mining in learning management systems.* Paper presented at the International Workshop on Applying Data Mining in e-Learning (ADML 2007), Crete, Greece.

Garrison, D. R., & Cleveland-Innes, M. (2005). Facilitating cognitive presence in online learning: Interaction is not enough. *The American Journal of Distance Education, 19*(3), 133–148.

Gibson, D., & Ifenthaler, D. (2017). Preparing the next generation of education researchers for Big Data in higher education. In B. K. Daniel (Ed.), *Big Data and Learning Analytics in higher education* (pp. 29–42). Switzerland: Springer International Publishing.

Gilbert, L., & Moore, D. R. (1998). Building interactivity into web courses: Tools for social and instructional interaction. *Educational Technology, 38*(3), 29–35.

Gokhale, A. A. (1995). Collaborative learning and critical thinking. *Journal of Technology Education, 7*, 22–30.

Graf, S., Liu, T.-C., & Kinshuk. (2010). Analysis of learners' navigational behaviour and their learning styles in an online course. *Journal of Computer Assisted Learning, 26*(2), 116–131. doi:10.1111/j.1365-2729.2009.00336.x

Greene, J. A., & Azevedo, R. (2010). The measurement of learners' self-regulated cognitive and metacognitive processes while using computer-based learning environments. *Educational Psychologist, 45*(4), 203–209.

Guerra, J., Sahebi, S., Lin, Y.-R., & Brusilovsky, P. (2014). *The problem solving genome: Analyzing sequential patterns of student work with parameterized exercises.* Paper presented at the 7th International Conference on Educational Data Mining, London. http://d-scholarship.pitt.edu/21805/

Gulbrandsen, C., Walsh, C. A., Fulton, A. E., Azulai, A., & Tong, H. (2015). Evaluating asynchronous discussion as social constructivist pedagogy in an online undergraduate gerontological social work course. *International Journal of Learning, Teaching and Educational Research, 10*(4), 94–111.

Guo, W. (2014, October). *From SPOC to MPOC--The effective practice of Peking University online teacher training.* Paper presented at the International Conference of Educational Innovation through Technology, Queensland, Australia.

Guo, W. W. (2010). Incorporating statistical and neural network approaches for student course satisfaction analysis and prediction. *Expert Systems with Applications, 37*(4), 3358–3365.

Harish, J. (2013). Online education: A revolution in the making. *Cadmus, 2*(1), 26.

Hay, A., Hodgkinson, M., Peltier, J. W., & Drago, W. A. (2004). Interaction and virtual learning. *Strategic Change, 13*(4), 193–204.

Haythornthwaite, C. (2001). Exploring Multiplexity: Social Network Structures in a Computer-Supported Distance Learning Class. *Information Society, 17*(3), 211–226.

Heckerman, D. (1998). A tutorial on learning with Bayesian networks. In M. Jordan (Ed.), *Proceedings of the NATO Advanced Study Institute on Learning in Graphical Models* (pp. 301–354). Springer Science+Business Media Dordrecht.

Hew, K. F. (2015). Student perceptions of peer versus instructor facilitation of asynchronous online discussions: further findings from three cases. *Instructional Science, 43*(1), 19–38.

Hew, K. F., & Cheung, W. S. (2014). Students' and instructors' use of massive open online courses (MOOCs): Motivations and challenges. *Educational Research Review, 12*, 45–58. doi:10.1016/j.edurev.2014.05.001

Hillman, D. C., Willis, D. J., & Gunawardena, C. N. (1994). Learner-interface interaction in distance education: An extension of contemporary models and strategies for practitioners. *American Journal of Distance Education, 8*(2), 30–42.

Hong, K.-S., Lai, K.-W., & Holton, D. (2003). Students' satisfaction and perceived learning with a web-based course. *Educational Technology & Society, 6*(1), 116–124.

Hou, H. T. (2012). Analyzing the Learning Process of an Online Role-Playing Discussion Activity. *Journal of Educational Technology & Society, 15*(1), 211–222.

Hou, H. T. (2015). Integrating cluster and sequential analysis to explore learners' flow and behavioral patterns in a simulation game with situated-learning context for science courses: A video-based process exploration. *Computers in Human Behavior, 48*, 424–435.

Huang, Y. (2014). *Structuring asynchronous online discussion groups: the impact of role-supported student facilitation.* University of Missouri--Columbia,

Inoue, Y., Ed. (2007). Online Education for Lifelong Learning. *Information Science Publishing, 8*(3), 341.

Jeong, H., Biswas, G., Johnson, J., & Howard, L. (2010). *Analysis of productive learning behaviors in a structured inquiry cycle using hidden Markov models.* Paper presented at the 3rd International Conference on Educational Data Mining, Pittsburgh, USA.

Jeong, H., Gupta, A., Roscoe, R., Wagster, J., Biswas, G., & Schwartz, D. (2008). *Using hidden Markov models to characterize student behaviors in learning-by-teaching environments.* Paper presented at the International Conference on Intelligent Tutoring Systems, Montreal, Canada.

Jonassen, D. H., & Kwon, H. (2001). Communication patterns in computer mediated versus face-to-face group problem solving. *Educational Technology Research & Development, 49*(1), 35–51.

Jung, I., Choi, S., Lim, C., & Leem, J. (2002). Effects of different types of interaction on learning achievement, satisfaction and participation in web-based instruction. *Innovations in education and teaching international, 39*(2), 153–162.

Kang, J., Liu, M., & Qu, W. (2017). Using gameplay data to examine learning behavior patterns in a serious game. *Computers in Human Behavior, 72*, 757–770. doi:10.1016/j.chb.2016.09.062

Kang, M., & Im, T. (2013). Factors of learner–instructor interaction which predict perceived learning outcomes in online learning environment. *Journal of Computer Assisted Learning, 29*(3), 292–301. doi:10.1111/jcal.12005

Kaplan, A. M., & Haenlein, M. (2016). Higher education and the digital revolution: About MOOCs, SPOCs, social media, and the Cookie Monster. *Business Horizons, 59*(4), 441–450. doi:10.1016/j.bushor.2016.03.008

Kay, J., Maisonneuve, N., Yacef, K., & Zaïane, O. (2006, June). *Mining patterns of events in students' teamwork data*. Paper presented at the Workshop on Educational Data Mining, the 8th International Conference on Intelligent Tutoring Systems, Jhongli, Taiwan, China.

Khalil, H., & Ebner, M. (2014, June). *MOOCs completion rates and possible methods to improve retention - A literature review*. Paper presented at the EdMedia: World Conference on Educational Multimedia, Hypermedia and Telecommunications, Tampere, Finland.

Kinnebrew, J. S., Loretz, K. M., & Biswas, G. (2013). A contextualized, differential sequence mining method to derive students' learning behavior patterns. *JEDM-Journal of Educational Data Mining, 5*(1), 190–219.

Klašnja-Milićević, A., Vesin, B., & Ivanović, M. (2018). Social tagging strategy for enhancing e-learning experience. *Computers & Education, 118*, 166–181. doi:10.101 6/j.compedu.2017.12.002

Koller, D., Ng, A., Do, C., & Chen, Z. (2013). Retention and intention in Massive Open Online Courses. *EDUCAUSE Review, 48*(3), 62.

Koschmann, T. D. (2001). *Revising the paradigms of instructional technolo*. Paper presented at the 8th Annual Conference of the Australasian Society for Computers in Learning in Tertiary Education (ASCILITE).

Koschmann, T. D., Myers, A. C., Feltovich, P. J., & Barrows, H. S. (1994). Using technology to assist in realizing effective learning and instruction: A principled approach to the use of computers in collaborative learning. *Journal of the Learning Sciences, 3*(3), 227–264.

Kuo, Y. C., Walker, A., Belland, B. R., & Schroder, K. E. E. (2014). A case study of integrating interwise: Interaction, internet self-efficacy, and satisfaction in synchronous online learning environments. *International Review of Research in Open & Distance Learning, 15*(1), 161–181.

Kuvalja, M., Kuvalja, M., Verma, M., Verma, M., Whitebread, D., & Whitebread, D. (2014). Patterns of co-occurring non-verbal behaviour and self-directed speech; a comparison of three methodological approaches. *Metacognition and learning, 9*(2), 87–111. doi:10.1007/s11409-013-9106-7

Kwong, S., He, Q., & Man, K. F. (1996). Training approach for hidden Markov models. *Electronics Letters, 32*(17), 1554–1555. doi:10.1049/el:19961080

Labaree, R. V. (2004). Issues in Web Based Pedagogy: A Critical Primer (review). *Review of Higher Education, 27*(2), 280–281.

Laesecke, A. (2002). Through measurement to knowledge: The inaugural lecture of Heike Kamerlingh Onnes. *Journal of Research of the National Institute of Standards and Technology, 107*, 261–277.

Larson, B. E., & Keiper, T. A. (2002). Classroom discussion and threaded electronic discussion: Learning in two arenas. *Contemporary Issues in Technology and Teacher Education, 2*(1), 45–62.

Larusson, J. A., & White, B. (2014). Introduction. In J. A. Larusson & B. White (Eds.), *Learning Analytics: From research to practice* (pp. 1–12). New York, NY: Springer Science+Business Media.

Leasure, A. R., Davis, L., & Thievon, S. L. (2000). Comparison of student outcomes and preferences in a traditional vs. world wide web-based baccalaureate nursing research course. *Journal of Nursing Education, 39*(4), 149–154.

Lehtinen, E. (2002). Developing models for distributed problem-based learning: Theoretical and methodological reflection. *Distance Education, 23*(1), 109–117.

Li, C., & Biswas, G. (2002). A Bayesian approach for structural learning with hidden Markov models. *Scientific Programming, 10*(3), 201–219.

Macfadyen, L. P., & Dawson, S. (2010). Mining LMS data to develop an "early warning system" for educators: A proof of concept. *Computers & Education, 54*(2), 588–599.

Macfadyen, L. P., Dawson, S., Pardo, A., & Gaševic, D. (2014). Embracing Big Data in complex educational systems: The Learning Analytics imperative and the policy challenge. *Research & Practice in Assessment, 9*, 17–28.

Magnusson, M. (2000). Discovering hidden time patterns in behavior: T-patterns and their detection. *Behavior Research Methods, Instruments, and Computers, 32*(1), 93–110.

Malmberg, J., Järvelä, S., & Järvenoja, H. (2017). Capturing temporal and sequential patterns of self-, co-, and socially shared regulation in the context of collaborative learning. *Contemporary Educational Psychology, 49*, 160–174. doi:10.1016/j.cedpsych.2017.01.009

Martinez, R., Yacef, K., Kay, J., Kharrufa, A., & Al-Qaraghuli, A. (2011). *Analysing frequent sequential patterns of collaborative learning activity around an interactive tabletop*. Paper presented at the 4th International Conference on Educational Data Mining, Eindhoven, Netherlands.

Mason, W., & Watts, D. J. (2012). Collaborative learning in networks. *Proceedings of the National Academy of Sciences, 109*(3), 764–769.

Mayer, R. E. (2008). *Learning and Instruction* (2nd ed.). New Jersey: Pearson.

McDonald, J. (2002). Is" as good as face-to-face" as good as it gets. *Journal of Asynchronous Learning Networks, 6*(2), 10–23.

Mercer, N. (2008). The seeds of time: Why classroom dialogue needs a temporal analysis. *Journal of the Learning Sciences, 17*(1), 33–59.

Meyer, E. (2015). Massive Open Online Courses (MOOCS): A Research Brief. doi: 10.13140/RG.2.1.4430.6406

Meyer, K. A. (2003). Face-to-face versus threaded discussions: The role of time and higher-order thinking. *Journal of Asynchronous Learning Networks, 7*(3), 55–65.

Molenaar, I. (2014). Advances in temporal analysis in learning and instruction. *Frontline Learning Research, 2*(4), 15–24.

Molenaar, I., & Chiu, M. M. (2014). Dissecting sequences of regulation and cognition: statistical discourse analysis of primary school children's collaborative learning. *Metacognition and learning, 9*, 137–160.

Moore, M. G. (1989). Editorial: Three types of interaction. *The American Journal of Distance Education, 3*(2), 1–6.

Moore, M. G., & Kearsley, G. (1996). *Distance education: A system view*. Belmont: Wadsworth Publishing Company.

Muhirwa, J.-M. (2009). Teaching and learning against all odds: A video-based study of learner-to-instructor interaction in international distance education. *The International Review of Research in Open and Distributed Learning, 10*(4).

Nesbit, J., Zhou, M., Xu, Y., & Winne, P. (2007). *Advancing log analysis of student interactions with cognitive tools*. Paper presented at the the 12th Biennial Conference of the European Association for Research on Learning and Instruction (EARLI), Budapest, Hungary.

Ni, A. Y. (2013). Comparing the effectiveness of classroom and online learning: Teaching research methods. *Journal of Public Affairs Education, 19*(2), 199–215.

Northrup, P., Lee, R., & Burgess, V. (2002). *Learner perceptions of online interaction.* Paper presented at the ED-MEDIA 2002 World Conference on Educational Multimedia, Hypermedia & Telecommunications, Denver, CO.

O'Malley, C. (2012). *Computer supported collaborative learning* (Vol. 128). Berlin: Springer Science & Business Media.

Ocumpaugh, J., Baker, R., Gowda, S., Heffernan, N., & Heffernan, C. (2014). Population validity for Educational Data Mining models: A case study in affect detection. *British Journal of Educational Technology, 45*(3), 487–501.

Palloff, R. M., & Pratt, K. (2002). *Lessons from the cyberspace classroom: The realities of online teaching.* John Wiley & Sons.

Panuccio, A., Bicego, M., & Murino, V. (2002). *A hidden Markov model-based approach to sequential data Clustering.* Paper presented at the Joint IAPR International Workshops on Statistical Techniques in Pattern Recognition, Windsor, Ontario, Canada.

Pardo, A. (2014). Designing Learning Analytics experiences. In J. A. Larusson & B. White (Eds.), *Learning Analytics: From research to practice* (pp. 15–38). New York, NY: Springer Science+Business Media.

Park, O. C., & Etgen, M. P. (2000). Research-based principles for multimedia presentation. In J. M. Spector & T. M. Anderson (Eds.), *Integrated and Holistic Perspectives on Learning Instruction and Technology* (pp. 197–212). London: Kluwer.

Park, Y., Yu, J. H., & Jo, I.-H. (2016). Clustering blended learning courses by online behavior data: A case study in a Korean higher education institute. *The Internet and Higher Education, 29*, 1–11.

Perera, D., Kay, J., Koprinska, I., Society, C., Yacef, K., & Zaïane, O. (2009). Clustering and sequential pattern mining of online collaborative learning data. *IEEE Transactions on Knowledge and Data Engineering, 21*(6), 759–772. doi:10.11 09/TKDE.2008.138

Perera, D., Kay, J., Koprinska, I., Yacef, K., & Zaïane, O. R. (2009). Clustering and sequential pattern mining of online collaborative learning data. *IEEE Transactions on Knowledge and Data Engineering, 21*(6), 759–772.

Perna, L. W., Ruby, A., Boruch, R. F., Wang, N., Scull, J., Ahmad, S., & Evans, C. (2014). Moving through MOOCs: Understanding the progression of users in massive open online courses. *Educational Researcher, 43*(9), 421–432.

Pham, T., University, V., & Dakich, E. (2014). Frequency and pattern of learner-instructor interaction in an online English language learning environment in Vietnam. *Australasian Journal of Educational Technology, 30*(6), 686–698.

Pinnell, C., Paulmani, G., & Kumar, V. (2017). Curricular and Learning Analytics: A Big Data perspective. In B. K. Daniel (Ed.), *Big Data and Learning Analytics in higher education* (pp. 125–145). Switzerland: Springer International Publishing.

Pistilli, M. D., Willis III, J. E., & Campbell, J. P. (2014). Analytics through an institutional lens: Definition, theory, design, and impact. In J. A. Larusson, & B. White (Eds.), *Learning Analytics: From research to practice* (pp. 79–102). New York, NY: Springer Science+Business Media.

Poole, M. S., van de Ven, A., Dooley, K., & Holmes, M. E. (2000). *Organizational change and innovation processes: Theories and methods for research.* New Oxford: Oxford University Press.

Psaromiligkos, Y., Orfanidou, M., Kytagias, C., & Zafiri, E. (2011). Mining log data for the analysis of learners' behaviour in web-based learning management systems. *Operational Research, 11*(2), 187–200.

Rabiner, L. R. (1989). A tutorial on hidden Markov models and selected applications in speech recognition. *Proceedings of the IEEE, 77*(2), 257–286.

Rabiner, L. R., & Juang, B. H. (1986). An introduction to hidden Markov models. *IEEE ASSP Magazine, 3*(1), 4–16.

Reimann, P. (2009). Time is precious: Variable- and event-centred approaches to process analysis in CSCL research. *International Journal of Computer-Supported Collaborative Learning, 4*(3), 239–257. doi:10.1007/s11412-009-9070-z

Reisetter, M., LaPointe, L., & Korcuska, J. (2007). The Impact of Altered Realties: Implications of Online Delivery for Learners' Interactions, Expectations, and Learning Skills. *International Journal on ELearning, 6*(1), 55.

Ritter, F. E., Nerb, J., Lehtinen, E., & O'Shea, T. M. (2007). *In order to learn: How the sequences of topics influences learning*. Oxford: Oxford University Press.

Roblyer, M. D., & Wiencke, W. R. (2003). Design and use of a rubric to assess and encourage interactive qualities in distance courses. *The American journal of distance education, 17*(2), 77–98.

Romero, C., González, P., Ventura, S., Del Jesús, M. J., & Herrera, F. (2009). Evolutionary algorithms for subgroup discovery in e-learning: A practical application using Moodle data. *Expert Systems with Applications, 36*(2), 1632–1644.

Romero, C., Romero, J. R., & Ventura, S. (2014). A survey on pre-processing educational data. In A. Peña-Ayala (Ed.), *Educational data mining* (pp. 29–64). Switzerland: Springer International Publishing.

Romero, C., Ventura, S., & García, E. (2008). Data mining in course management systems: Moodle case study and tutorial. *Computers & Education, 51*(1), 368–384.

Russell, T. L. (1999). *The no significant difference phenomenon: As reported in 355 research reports, summaries and papers*: North Carolina State University.

Sabry, K., & Baldwin, L. (2003). Web-based learning interaction and learning styles. *British Journal of Educational Technology, 34*(4), 443–454.

Sargeant, J., Curran, V., Allen, M., Jarvis-Selinger, S., & Ho, K. (2006). Facilitating interpersonal interaction and learning online: Linking theory and practice. *The Journal of Continuing Education in the Health Professions, 26*(2), 128–136.

Schmitz, B. (2006). Advantages of studying processes in educational research. *Learning and Instruction, 16*(5), 433–449.

Schwarz, G. (1978). Estimating the dimension of a model. *Annals of Statistics, 6*(2), 461–464.

Siemens, G., & Long, P. (2011). Penetrating the fog: Analytics in learning and education. *EDUCAUSE Review, 46*(4), 31–40.

Sinha, N., Khreisat, L., & Sharma, K. (2009). Learner-interface interaction for technology-enhanced active learning. *Innovate Journal of Online Education, 5*(3), 1–7.

Skog, T. K. (2010). Learner Satisfaction in Online Learning. *Quarterly Review of Distance Education, 8*(3), 192–193.

Smyth, R. (2011). Enhancing learner–learner interaction using video communications in higher education: Implications from theorising about a new model. *British Journal of Educational Technology, 42*(1), 113–127.

Snyder, T. D., de Brey, C., & Dillow, S. A. (2016). *Digest of education statistics 2014*. Washington, DC: National Center for Education Statistics, Institute of Education Sciences, U.S. Department of Education.

Soller, A., & Lesgold, A. (2007). Modeling the process of collaborative learning. In H. U. Hoppe, H. Ogata, & A. Soller (Eds.), *The role of technology in CSCL* (Vol. 9, pp. 63–86). Boston, MA: Springer.

Soo, K.-S., & Bonk, C. J. (1998). Interaction: What Does It Mean in Online Distance Education? Retrieved from https://eric.ed.gov/?id=ED428724

Stahl, G. (2010). Group cognition: Computer support for building collaborative knowledge. *Journal of the Association for Information Science & Technology, 59*(9), 1531-1531.

Sun, J. C.-Y., Hwang, G.-J., Lin, Y.-Y., Yu, S.-J., Pan, L.-C., & Chen, A. Y.-Z. (2018). A votable concept mapping approach to promoting students' attentional behavior: An analysis of sequential behavioral patterns and brainwave data. *Journal of Educational Technology & Society, 21*(2), 177–191.

Sung, Y. T., Hou, H. T., Liu, C. K., & Chang, K. E. (2010). Mobile guide system using problem-solving strategy for museum learning: a sequential learning behavioural pattern analysis. *Journal of Computer Assisted Learning, 26*(2), 106–115. doi:10.1111/j.1365-2729.2010.00345.x

Swan, K. (2001). Virtual interaction: Design factors affecting student satisfaction and perceived learning in asynchronous online courses. *Distance Education, 22*, 306–331.

Swan, K. (2004). Learning online: current research on issues of interface, teaching presence and learner characteristics. In J. Bourne & J. C. Moore (Eds.), *Elements of quality online education, into the mainstream* (pp. 63–79). Needham, MA: Sloan Center for Online Education.

Talavera, L., & Gaudioso, E. (2004, August). *Mining student data to characterize similar behavior groups in unstructured collaboration spaces.* Paper presented at the Workshop on Artificial Intelligence in CSCL, the 16th European Conference on Artificial Intelligence (ECAI 2004), Valencia, Spain.

Thomas, J. (2013). Exploring the use of asynchronous online discussion in health care education: A literature review. *Computers & Education, 69*, 199–215.

Thurmond, V. A. (2003). *Examination of interaction variables as predictors of students' satisfaction and willingness to enroll in future Web-based courses while controlling for student characteristics.* (Doctoral dissertation), University of Kansas, Retrieved from ProQuest Dissertations Publishing. (UMI No. 3111497)

Thurmond, V. A., & Wambach, K. (2004). Understanding interactions in distance education: A review of the literature. *International Journal of Instructional Technology and Distance Learning, 1*(1), 9–26.

Trentin, G. (1998). Computer Conferencing Systems as Seen by a Designer of Online Courses. *Educational Technology, 38*(3), 36–43.

Veenman, M. V. J. (2011). Learning to self-monitor and self-regulate. In R. Mayer & P. Alexander (Eds.), *Handbook of research on learning and instruction* (pp. 197–218). New York: Routledge.

Venant, R., Sharma, K., Vidal, P., Dillenbourg, P., & Broisin, J. (2017). *Using sequential pattern mining to explore learners' behaviors and evaluate their correlation with performance in inquiry-based learning.* Paper presented at the European Conference on Technology Enhanced Learning, Tallinn, Estonia.

Vrasidas, C., & McIsaac, M. S. (1999). Factors influencing interaction in an online course. *American Journal of Distance Education, 13*(3), 22–36. doi:10.1080/08923649909527033

Vygotsky, L. S. (1978). *Mind in society: The development of higher psychological processes* (M. Cole, V. John-Steiner, S. Schribner, & E. Souberman, Trans. M. Cole, V. John-Steiner, S. Schribner, & E. Souberman Eds.). Cambridge, MA: Harvard University Press.

Wagner, E. D. (1994). In support of a functional definition of interaction. *American Journal of Distance Education, 8*(2), 6–29.

Wanstreet, C. E. (2006). Interaction in online learning environments: A review of the literature. *The Quarterly Review of Distance Education, 7*(4), 399–411.

Wilson, B. G. (2004). Designing E-Learning environments for flexible activity and instruction. *Educational Technology Research and Development, 52*(4), 77–84. doi: 10.1007/BF02504720

Witten, I. H., & Frank, E. (1999). Data mining: Practical machine learning tools and techniques with Java implementations. *Acm Sigmod Record, 31*(1), 76–77.

Woods, R. H., & Baker, J. D. (2004). Interaction and immediacy in online learning. *The International Review of Research in Open and Distributed Learning, 5*(2), 13.

Yacci, M. (2000). Interactivity demystified: A structural definition for distance education and intelligent computer-based instruction. *Educational Technology, 40*, 5–16.

You, J. W. (2016). Identifying significant indicators using LMS data to predict course achievement in online learning. *Internet and Higher Education, 29*, 23–30.

Zhang, D. (2005). Interactive multimedia-based e-learning: A study of effectiveness. *The American Journal of Distance Education, 19*(3), 149–162.

Zheng, J., Xing, W., & Zhu, G. (2019). Examining sequential patterns of self- and socially shared regulation of STEM learning in a CSCL environment. *Computers & Education, 136*, 34–48. doi:10.1016/j.compedu.2019.03.005

Zimmerman, T. D. (2012). Exploring learner to content interaction as a success factor in online courses. *International Review of Research in Open & Distance Learning, 13*(4), 151–165.

5 Massive Private Open Courses

MOOCs vs MPOCs

In online learning, there are different organizational forms that provide interaction data with different qualities. Kaplan and Haenlein (2016) summarized that there are two representative forms of online learning being conducted at present: MOOCs and SPOCs. A MOOC is an open-access online course (i.e., without specific participation restrictions) that allows for unlimited (massive) participation; many MOOCs provide interactive elements to encourage interactions among learners and between learners and the teaching staff (Kaplan & Haenlein, 2016). An SPOC is an online course that only offers a limited number of places and therefore requires some form of formal enrollment; SPOCs frequently have a competitive application process and might charge a tuition fee (Kaplan & Haenlein, 2016). MOOCs and SPOCs differ primarily in the sizes of the learner populations to which they cater.

However, Kaplan and Haenlein (2016) ignore another important online learning organization form, MPOCs, massive private online courses. An MPOC is a massive private online course designed on the model of SPOC in conventional distance-learning settings. In MPOCs, online facilitators are assigned to the online classes to lead online trainees to fulfill the online learning activities, assess their achievements, and provide timely feedback to learners (Guo, 2014). MPOCs offer a limited number of enrollments like SPOCs, but because of the lower tuitions, the size of online classes in MPOCs is big and the enrollments of learners are massive (Guo, 2014). For example, in a training program conducted by Peking University in China, from 2007–2013, nearly 500,000 k-12 teachers had enrolled in this online training course in about 5,000 online classes, with approximately 2,000 online facilitators who had also joined the online practice (Guo, 2014). This program is a typical MPOC form of online learning.

Unlike MOOCs, conventional online and distance-learning courses are not intended to be 'open' to users moving in and out of a course multiple times (Perna et al., 2014). MPOCs, like China's Open University or Turkey's Anadolu University, are characterized as more uniform, regulated, and

DOI: 10.4324/b23163-6

centralized than MOOCs. Although MOOCs mean massive open online courses, because of the extremely high dropout rate (more than 95%) and loose organization in MOOCs, most learners' interaction trace data are not actually present throughout the entire course process (Hew & Cheung, 2014). This means that the final complete data in MOOCs are not that massive, nor complete. Further, many MPOCs conducted by conventional online institutions cannot only accumulate relatively complete data of learner interaction such as views of specific resources, attempts and completion of quizzes, or discussion messages viewed or posted, but also record the demographic information and the previous learning status of their learners. Therefore, MPOCs can provide more comprehensive data than MOOCs to investigate the interaction details in online learning.

However, given that MOOCs have attracted all the attention in online learning, little research has been conducted so far to understand how different achievement learners learn in today's MPOCs and how learners, instructors, institutions, and researchers can best support their learning process.

Comparative Research of Interaction Patterns, the Lack of MPOCs

The final purpose of a course, no matter in MOOCs or MPOCs, is to improve the knowledge and skills of all learners. The first step, also the prerequisite, is learners who take the course have to stay in the course. Only when they stay in the course, can they interact with material, instructors, and peers, and learn new knowledge and skills. The second important step is to investigate effective ways to improve learning. Comparing the interaction differences between high-achievement learners and low-achievement learners is one of the ways to discover some effective learner interaction patterns from strong learners, which can help to facilitate other learners (Jeong, Biswas, Johnson, & Howard, 2010; Martinez, Yacef, Kay, Kharrufa, & Al-Qaraghuli, 2011; Perera, Kay, Koprinska, Yacef, & Zaïane, 2009).

However, in MOOCs, only a few learners finally persist (stay and learn) or complete (pass the final exam) the courses (Hew & Cheung, 2014; Khalil & Ebner, 2014; Koller, Ng, Do, & Chen, 2013). Almost all the focus of MOOCs is on learner retention and persistence (de Freitas, Morgan, & Gibson, 2015; Hew & Cheung, 2014; Khalil & Ebner, 2014; Koller et al., 2013; Meyer, 2015), which means research in MOOCs is still in an initial stage with regard to learning outcomes, but, fortunately, without these dropout issues, MPOCs research has already moved on to the second step.

Moreover, there is an increasing demand for skilled and trained citizens in this competitive world; colleges and universities face increased demand from the workforce sector where ongoing up-skilling and re-training is required to maintain employment in a rapidly changing economic, social, and technical world (Dolence & Norris, 1995). However, educational institutions are finding it difficult to graduate learners who can meet the requirements

(Bomatpalli, 2014). Fortunately, learners in MPOCs are more engaged, active, persistent, and goal-oriented, and therefore, their learning is more effective. They will be more employable, and they deserve particular concern from institutions and researchers.

There is little doubt that as learners in MPOCs maintain a high persistence rate – from the beginning to the end of the course process – the generation of huge quantities of learning-related data is also uninterrupted and of high quality. If studies in MPOCs follow the trends that target fine-grained interaction data, there will be a widespread interest in how these valuable data could be used to improve learning and teaching in MPOCs settings.

A key issue is how to leverage these data to clarify what different learners understand and how they conduct learning, to derive meaningful measures of different learning processes, and to develop capabilities for precise diagnosis and targeting of instruction.

The belief of this study is that certain sequences of interaction events may distinguish the strong groups from the weak ones. Kinnebrew and colleagues (2013) summarized four ways to analyze LMS trace data: (i) frequency of studying events, (ii) patterns of studying activity, (iii) timing and sequencing of events, and (iv) content analyses of learners' notes and summaries (Kinnebrew, Loretz, & Biswas, 2013). Frequency, static patterns, and content analysis are easier to be accepted based on the knowledge of traditional statistics, but an important aspect of trace data that has been greatly ignored is the timing and sequence. Perera and colleagues (2009) insisted that certain sequence patterns of interaction can distinguish better learners from the weaker ones (Perera et al., 2009).

Excepting the general interaction sequences shared in all groups, some interaction sequences may be more common in the traces of high-achievement learners and much less in low-achievement learners; while other interaction sequences may be more common in low-achievement learners' traces and less in high-achievement learners' traces. Interaction sequence patterns in the high-achievement group may have the potential for helping low-achievement learners to improve their own performance (Kay, Maisonneuve, Yacef, & Zaïane, 2006). In other words, if a learner appears to have many patterns associated with risks, the learner should be reminded; if there is a rise in the patterns associated with success, it may facilitate learners to improve achievements.

Comparative research can help in measuring learner interaction, acquiring the skills to succeed, and promoting academic success in MPOCs. With comparison analysis, this study steps beyond the inquiry of whether learners stay and construct knowledge in LMSs, and investigates when and how learners interact through LMSs to conduct their knowledge. Moving forward, it will help improve all learners' learning with new insight and depth, while at the same time producing new types of information that provoke new questions about learning experiences in MPOCs.

Summary

Interaction if the foundation of learning. Researchers have done much useful work to define interaction as a framework and identify a theoretical basis for the characteristics of interaction associated with online learning (Chen, 2004; Gilbert & Moore, 1998; Mayer, 2008; Moore, 1989; Roblyer & Wiencke, 2003; Vrasidas & McIsaac, 1999; Wagner, 1994; Yacci, 2000).

Learning is a process full of interaction to gain skills and knowledge; also, it can be recognized through changes in the learners' behaviors (Mayer, 2008; Vygotsky, 1978). Because it takes learners time to acquire skills and knowledge, and learning behaviors always change sequentially, the concept of time and sequence is innate to learning (Molenaar, 2014). However, in previous interaction studies, researchers mostly employed traditional statistical methods, which capture time in pre-test and post-test designs and ignore sequences changing in shorter time spans. As such they often focused on a narrow concept of relations between interaction entities such as content, instructors, peers, and interfaces (Hillman, Willis, & Gunawardena, 1994; Moore, 1989); therefore, these studies reduce the validity and explanatory power of interaction research. Currently, technology advancements in LMSs and digital APPs increase the ability to gain huge amounts of behavior traces of learners while they are interacting with the devices, which is an important facilitator to overcome previous issues of lack of knowledge about time and sequence (Reimann, 2009).

Recently, more and more researchers have begun to address how different learning behaviors act and develop over time (Baker & Siemens, 2014; Molenaar & Chiu, 2014; Reimann, 2009). Also, they have conceptualized behaviors in learning processes in many ways, leading to a diverse set of dimensions of research questions at the micro-level (Molenaar, 2014). Temporal and sequential analysis entails a new methodology, learning analytics, which deviates from previous statistical research methods, changing our analysis from statics outcomes of learning performance and demographic information to dynamic process characteristics of learning behaviors. There are two kinds of research questions. The first one focuses on the dynamic process data themselves. For example, which sequences of learner behaviors occur during learning and instruction? The other one combines temporal and sequential characteristics with static outcome information such as learning performance or course achievement. For example, which patterns of interaction during learning influence course achievement positively? Research has illustrated that learning analytics and big data in LMSs can support the transparency of interaction behaviors and enhance the comparability of different learners' performances.

The final goal of this line of time and sequence research is to offer adapted support and direct feedback to learners or to their facilitators in real daily course work under online settings (Martinez et al., 2011). However, given the challenges to coordinate many complicated factors in the massive online learners, long-term learning process, non-experiment environment, and huge data files, most of the studies have been conducted in small groups under MOOCs, higher education, and K-12 settings. MPOCs has been ignored by most researchers.

This study focuses on LMS data and learning analytics approaches to make sense of different interaction behaviors occurring in different MPOCs groups. It can provide detailed information on learner interaction such as the sequence of accessing online resources and activities, the rate at which learners advance through the learning process, and the amount of time spent examining resources (Antonenko, Toy, & Niederhauser, 2012). Also, it can help establish and compare patterns of different learner interactions in different groups based on their interactions with materials, instructors, and peers in MPOCs.

On the other side, this study is an exploration of the paradigm shift of the research methodology. First, it focuses on the temporal and sequential characteristics of interaction to find out which meaningful sequences of learning activities occur during learning and instruction. Second, it combines the activity patterns with the final course achievement which is a kind of static outcome information commonly used in variable-based research. The purpose of this combination is to identify which patterns of interaction influence course achievement positively or not.

Chen (2004) clarified that there are two roles of learner-centered interaction in online learning: one is to change the behavior of learners, and the other is to facilitate the learners' behavior to gradually approach the learning objectives. This study investigates some 'no-easy-answer' questions, such as whether high achievement groups behave differently from low achievement groups, and whether learners' interaction activity patterns change in different course processes.

References

Antonenko, P. D., Toy, S., & Niederhauser, D. S. (2012). Using cluster analysis for data mining in educational technology research. *Educational Technology Research and Development*, *60*(3), 383–398.

Baker, R., & Siemens, G. (2014). Educational data mining and learning analytics. In K. Sawyer (Ed.), *Cambridge handbook of the learning sciences* (2nd ed., pp. 253–274). New York, NY: Cambridge University Press.

Bomatpalli, T. (2014). Learning analytics and big data in higher education. *International Journal of Engineering Research & Technology*, *3*(1), 3377–3383.

Chen, L. (2004). An investigation into "Interactivity" and the related concepts. *China Distance Education*, *3*, 12–19.

de Freitas, S. I., Morgan, J., & Gibson, D. (2015). Will MOOCs transform learning and teaching in higher education? Engagement and course retention in online learning provision. *British Journal of Educational Technology*, *46*(3), 455–471.

Dolence, M. G., & Norris, D. M. (1995). *Transforming higher education: A vision for learning in the 21st century*. Ann Arbor, MI: Society for College and University Planning.

Gilbert, L., & Moore, D. R. (1998). Building interactivity into web courses: Tools for social and instructional interaction. *Educational Technology, 38*(3), 29–35.

Guo, W. (2014, October). *From SPOC to MPOC–The effective practice of Peking University online teacher training*. Paper presented at the International Conference of Educational Innovation through Technology, Queensland, Australia.

Hew, K. F., & Cheung, W. S. (2014). Students' and instructors' use of massive open online courses (MOOCs): Motivations and challenges. *Educational Research Review, 12*, 45–58. doi:10.1016/j.edurev.2014.05.001

Hillman, D. C., Willis, D. J., & Gunawardena, C. N. (1994). Learner-interface interaction in distance education: An extension of contemporary models and strategies for practitioners. *American Journal of Distance Education, 8*(2), 30–42.

Jeong, H., Biswas, G., Johnson, J., & Howard, L. (2010). *Analysis of productive learning behaviors in a structured inquiry cycle using hidden Markov models*. Paper presented at the 3rd International Conference on Educational Data Mining, Pittsburgh, USA.

Kaplan, A. M., & Haenlein, M. (2016). Higher education and the digital revolution: About MOOCs, SPOCs, social media, and the Cookie Monster. *Business Horizons, 59*(4), 441–450. doi: 10.1016/j.bushor.2016.03.008

Kay, J., Maisonneuve, N., Yacef, K., & Zaïane, O. (2006, June). *Mining patterns of events in students' teamwork data*. Paper presented at the Workshop on Educational Data Mining, the 8th International Conference on Intelligent Tutoring Systems, Jhongli, Taiwan, China.

Khalil, H., & Ebner, M. (2014, June). *MOOCs completion rates and possible methods to improve retention - A literature review*. Paper presented at the EdMedia: World Conference on Educational Multimedia, Hypermedia and Telecommunications, Tampere, Finland.

Kinnebrew, J. S., Loretz, K. M., & Biswas, G. (2013). A contextualized, differential sequence mining method to derive students' learning behavior patterns. *JEDM-Journal of Educational Data Mining, 5*(1), 190–219.

Koller, D., Ng, A., Do, C., & Chen, Z. (2013). Retention and intention in Massive Open Online Courses. *EDUCAUSE Review, 48*(3), 62.

Martinez, R., Yacef, K., Kay, J., Kharrufa, A., & Al-Qaraghuli, A. (2011). *Analysing frequent sequential patterns of collaborative learning activity around an interactive tabletop*. Paper presented at the 4th International Conference on Educational Data Mining, Eindhoven, Netherlands.

Mayer, R. E. (2008). *Learning and Instruction* (2nd ed.). New Jersey: Pearson.

Meyer, E. (2015). Massive Open Online Courses (MOOCS): A Research Brief. doi: 10.13140/RG.2.1.4430.6406

Molenaar, I. (2014). Advances in temporal analysis in learning and instruction. *Frontline Learning Research, 2*(4), 15–24.

Molenaar, I., & Chiu, M. M. (2014). Dissecting sequences of regulation and cognition: Statistical discourse analysis of primary school children's collaborative learning. *Metacognition and Learning, 9*, 137–160.

Moore, M. G. (1989). Editorial: Three types of interaction. *The American Journal of Distance Education, 3*(2), 1–6.

Perera, D., Kay, J., Koprinska, I., Yacef, K., & Zaïane, O. R. (2009). Clustering and sequential pattern mining of online collaborative learning data. *IEEE Transactions on Knowledge and Data Engineering, 21*(6), 759–772.

Perna, L. W., Ruby, A., Boruch, R. F., Wang, N., Scull, J., Ahmad, S., & Evans, C. (2014). Moving through MOOCs: Understanding the progression of users in massive open online courses. *Educational Researcher, 43*(9), 421–432.

Reimann, P. (2009). Time is precious: Variable- and event-centred approaches to process analysis in CSCL research. *International Journal of Computer-Supported Collaborative Learning, 4*(3), 239–257. doi:10.1007/s11412-009-9070-z

Roblyer, M. D., & Wiencke, W. R. (2003). Design and use of a rubric to assess and encourage interactive qualities in distance courses. *The American Journal of Distance Education, 17*(2), 77–98.

Vrasidas, C., & McIsaac, M. S. (1999). Factors influencing interaction in an online course. *American Journal of Distance Education, 13*(3), 22–36. doi:10.1080/08923 649909527033

Vygotsky, L. S. (1978). *Mind in society: The development of higher psychological processes* (M. Cole, V. John-Steiner, S. Schribner, & E. Souberman, Trans. M. Cole, V. John-Steiner, S. Schribner, & E. Souberman Eds.). Cambridge, MA: Harvard University Press.

Wagner, E. D. (1994). In support of a functional definition of interaction. *American Journal of Distance Education, 8*(2), 6–29.

Yacci, M. (2000). Interactivity demystified: A structural definition for distance education and intelligent computer-based instruction. *Educational Technology, 40*, 5–16.

6 Research Design of a MPOCs Case

Background and Research Questions

Learner interaction is one of the most important factors related to learning, which is the foundation of a successful learning experience, especially in online learning. However, decoding the sequence patterns of online interaction is the research weakness in many online learning studies. Further, learner interaction traces in LMSs logs and the learning analytics methodology, which is a valuable resource to identify interaction patterns in online learning, are also overlooked. Most researchers in online learning would not disagree that LMSs log data and learning analytics are really required because there is an on-going need to make the 'black box' of learner interaction become visible, decode the secret of complex interaction behaviors, and help all the learners effectively achieve their learning purpose in online settings.

In addition, most of the research in online learning is still restricted to the narrow context within specific retention issues in MOOCs. To date, little research has been conducted so far to understand how learners at different achievement levels learn in MPOCs, and how learners, instructors, institutions, and researchers can best support their learning process. Efforts to attract more research attention into MPOCs must focus on the learner interaction research and identify dynamic interaction patterns, such as the activity patterns and the action patterns in different achievement groups, and the development of interaction activities through different course processes.

This study enables a new perspective of the data-driven research into online learning and makes it possible to gain highly detailed insight into learner interaction at the micro-level. In the short term, it is helpful to discover and compare dynamic interaction behaviors of different learner groups in MPOCs, and to determine which patterns are associated with better overall learning and which sequences are indicative of problems. In the long term, it is helpful to provide an attempt to employ learning analytics to learner interaction research, to provide opportunities for learners to gain insight into and evaluate their own learning, to help instructors identify

DOI: 10.4324/b23163-7

at-risk learners and adjust instructional strategies, and to contribute to MPOCs institutional effectiveness, highlighting of MPOCs successes, and increasing organizational productivity.

The aim of this study is to employ learning analytics to the log data in MPOCs and build comparison analyses summarizing interaction patterns. The context is an 20 weeks Moodle-based course, which occurred over a long and uninterrupted learning process in a whole semester. The course took place as part of a mandatory subject in the third year of a computer degree program at an open university in China. The general research purpose is to contribute to the knowledge of interaction patterns by comparing interaction activities in different achievement groups in MPOCs. With this purpose, four research questions are set:

1. Are the interaction activity patterns of High-achievement learners' group and Low-achievement learners' group the same or different in Learning weeks?
2. Are the interaction activity patterns of High-achievement learners' group and Low-achievement learners' group the same or different in Exam weeks?
3. Does the interaction activity pattern of High-achievement learners' group remain the same from Learning weeks to Exam weeks?
4. Does the interaction activity pattern of Low-achievement learners' group remain unchanged from Learning weeks to Exam weeks?

In our study line, online learners' interaction behaviors are clarified at two levels: interaction activity level and interaction action level. An interaction activity is defined as a sequence of learner interaction behaviors within one LMS module. For example, in Moodle, corresponding to the modules, interaction activities may include Introduction, Content, Forum, Quiz, Assignment, and so on. An interaction action is defined as the educationally meaningful typical behavior in an interaction activity such as view, delete, change, and create, and so on. This study focuses on the learners' interaction activity.

After setting the research questions and clarifying the key terms, the participants and data collection are described. The methodology is then described in two different phases. In the first stage, data pre-processing is conducted; in the second stage, HMMs are employed to address the four research questions.

Participants and Data Collection

The context is a 20-week Moodle-based online course, *Basis of Computer Applications*. This course is part of a mandatory subject in a computer degree program of a traditional open university in one of the Chinese provinces, which is for beginners with some basic skills in computer applications. The designers and instructors adopt an exploratory learning mode of 'learning by doing' to build a virtual software operating environment for learners, which aims to help learners learn the basic knowledge and skills of the Windows operating system, and Internet, MS office software, and computer security. The first 16 weeks are Learning weeks; the last four weeks are Exam weeks. In 2018, initial enrollment in the course included 1490 learners, and 1375 students took the course exam and finished the course.

There are eight Moodle activity modules:

1. Introduction & Announcement, where learners get the course description and messages;
2. Content, where learners learn the seven course-chapters;
3. Resource, which includes frequently asked questions about the content, experiment guides, simulated tests of the final exam, and different types of materials to improve learners learning;
4. Assignment & Quiz, which is for learners to consolidate their learning;
5. Performance statement, where learners check their own and their peers' performance;
6. Forum, where learners discuss with instructors and peers; Instructors especially emphasize discussions in the forum, but discussions are not included in the final grade of the course;
7. Group learning, where learners conduct projects in a group; there are three occasions for mandatory group learning in Learning weeks;
8. Course evaluation, where learners evaluate their instructors, peers and the course after they finish the course.

For each learner, Moodle sequentially records the information of learners' interaction activity in real time throughout the whole semester as well as the grade of the final exam.

To answer the research questions, different sources of data in the course are collected after learners worked through the semester, such as their final marks and the interaction traces in the LMS. The final grades for the semester can be used to look for interaction patterns that are more or less commonly performed among different achievement learner groups: patterns more common for strong groups may be indicators of success, and patterns more common for weak groups may be indicators of problems. This type of research is seeking to provide ways in which learners' interactions with various entities can be captured, interrelated, analyzed, and understood in terms of some typical interaction patterns.

Data Pre-processing and Analysis

The first and one of the key steps to making data useful for analysis is data pre-processing (Romero, Romero, & Ventura, 2014). Data pre-processing is the process of engineering and distilling appropriate features that can be used to represent key aspects of the data, which is one of the most time-consuming and difficult steps in learning analytics (García, Romero, Ventura, & Calders, 2007). The two main families of techniques are detection techniques to find imperfections in data sets, and transforming techniques oriented to obtain more manageable data sets (Romero et al., 2014).

Base on the suggestions from Romero and colleagues (2008), there are two tasks for the data pre-processing in this study:

Create summarization tables: to create a new table in the Moodle database that can summarize information of each learner. As learner and interaction data are spread over several tables, a summary table will integrate the most important information for answering the research questions. This table (mdl_sum) has a summary per row about all the activities done by each learner during the course and the final mark obtained by the learner in the course.

Transform the data: the data must be transformed into the required format of the Learning analytics algorithm or framework. To investigate frequently occurring activity sequence patterns in different achievement groups, the mdl_sum table will be first divided into two datasets: High-achievement group and Low-achievement group by grade C based on the final course grade. Grade C is used as the dividing line because, based on the regulations of the open university, learners with grade C or higher are the ones passing the course, learners with grades lower than C are the ones failing the course. Thus, in this course, there are 974 learners in the High-achievement group (grade>=C), and 401 learners in the Low-achievement group (grade<C). Finally, given on grade C and two course-processes (Learning process, Exam process), researchers have four datasets: High-Learning, Low-Learning, High-Exam, and Low-Exam (please see Table 6.1).

There are eight activity modules in the Moodle course, and the sequences of these activities are extracted from the log files and then pre-processed. The goal is to determine if there is evidence of different activity patterns between two achievement groups during the course process and whether these patterns change when learners worked in the different course sessions.

Table 6.1 Four datasets

	Learning weeks (16 weeks)	*Exam weeks (four weeks)*
High-achievement	High-Learning (n = 974, grade >= C)	High-Exam (n = 974, grade >= C)
Low-achievement	Low-Learning (n = 401, grade < C)	Low-Exam (n = 401, grade < C)

HMMs Measures[1]

In this study, learners' interaction activity pattern is defined as the sequence of indirect interaction states in a certain course process; these patterns are frequently performed among high and low achievement groups. Based on the literature, HMMs (Rabiner & Juang, 1986) is the specific approach employed in this study, which is a probabilistic state-based approach to generate indirect state patterns based on direct activity sequences (Bahl, Brown, De Souza, & Mercer, 1986; Ben-Yishai & Burshtein, 2004; Jeong et al., 2008; Kwong, He, & Man, 1996; Li & Biswas, 2002; Panuccio, Bicego, & Murino, 2002; Rabiner, 1989; Rabiner & Juang, 1986; Soller & Lesgold, 2007). Here, the key parameters and procedures of HMMs are introduced. For the details of HMMs algorithm, please see Appendix in this study.

HMMs manifests the hidden states through three sets of parameters (Bahl et al., 1986; Ben-Yishai & Burshtein, 2004; Kwong et al., 1996; Li & Biswas, 2002; Rabiner, 1989).

Initial probability vector π: initial probabilities for hidden activity states. An initial probability represents the chance of learners engaging in a particular hidden activity state during a given course process.

Transition probability matrix, A: the transition probabilities between each of the hidden activity states;

> Output probability matrix, B: observation activity probabilities for detecting a particular observation activity in a hidden activity state. An observation activity probability represents the proportion of learner engagement of an observable activity in a given hidden state because that hidden state may consist of several observable activities.

The meaning or interpretation of a particular hidden state is based on the interaction activities associated with that hidden state (Jeong et al., 2008).

HMMs algorithm tries to derive an optimal set of the parameters (π, A, B), which can maximize the likelihood of the input activity sequences (Bahl et al., 1986; Ben-Yishai & Burshtein, 2004; Kwong et al., 1996). Given each dataset, the input activity sequence in HMMs is learners' observable sequential interaction activities from the beginning to the end in a certain course process. Take the dataset of High-Learning as an example: Here the input activity sequence is the High-achievement learners' sequential activities recorded in real time by LMS from Week one to Week 16, and the sample size is 974 (please see Table 6.1).

The first step is to initialize the parameters that define the states and the possible state transitions (Li & Biswas, 2002; Rabiner, 1989). The well-known *Baum-Welch* (BW) method, a variation of the general expectation-maximization (EM), is employed to estimate the three sets of parameters (π, A, B) in HMMs (Baum, Petrie, Soules, & Weiss, 1970; Ben-Yishai & Burshtein, 2004; Martinez, Yacef, Kay, Kharrufa, & Al-Qaraghuli, 2011). Particularly, to improve the accuracy of the parameter values in the BW procedure, the *Viterbi* algorithm is the way of starting with initial parameter values that are better than random (Li & Biswas, 2002).

Another issue to define HMMs is the 'best' number of hidden activity states to model the data (Heckerman, 1998; Li & Biswas, 2002; Schwarz, 1978). To gain an educationally interpretable simple model, the Bayesian information criterion (BIC) is used to achieve a balance between 'high likelihood' which means how likely the model fits the data and 'low complexity' which means the number of the states in the derived model (Heckerman, 1998; Schwarz, 1978).

BIC is a well-established and easily interpretable method for model selection, which is derived from the Laplace approximation (Li & Biswas, 2002). BIC computation is $-\log(L)+(d/2)\log(N)$ (Schwarz, 1978). The first term, $-\log(L)$, is the likelihood term which tends to favor larger and more detailed models of data; the second term, $(d/2)\log(N)$, is the model complexity penalty term; d represents the number of significant parameters in the model, which is influenced by the number of the hidden states; N represents the sample size. The best number of hidden states is indicated by the smallest value of BIC (Heckerman, 1998; Li & Biswas, 2002; Schwarz, 1978).

HMMs Procedures

In this study, HMMs have been run in the four different datasets: High-Learning, Low-Learning, High-Exam, and Low-Exam. Then, there will be four models resulting from the HMMs algorithm. The HMMs offer a state-based aggregated interpretation of learners' activity sequences, which can be analyzed in various ways (Jeong, Biswas, Johnson, & Howard, 2010; Jeong et al., 2008):

Each model is made up of a set of states; some states may represent a single activity, others may comprise more than one activity, and each state will be labeled by the predominant activity (or activities) present in that state (Jeong et al., 2010). The major activities are identified by the proportion of time spent in each activity. Naming each discrete state is helpful to provide evidence to determine what interaction activities these states indicate.

Further, transition probabilities between two states provide the likelihoods (expressed as a percentage) of learners transitioning to different states or remaining in the current state (Jeong et al., 2010). The transitions between states give a sense of how learners transition between different interaction activities.

In addition, the stationary probability gives a sense of what states frequently occur in a session. The stationary probability is the relative proportion of activities that belongs to a certain state; for example, a state with a 20% stationary probability implies that 20% of learners' activities during the session are related to the interaction activities in the state (Jeong et al., 2010).

The HMMs results are compared and analyzed within the new framework of learner interaction. The probability of activity time spending in each state indicates the major activities in the state, which is also the name of the state. The transition probability (the transition likelihood) indicates the likelihood of learner interaction staying in the current sate or transitioning from the current state to the different indicated state(s). The comparison of these patterns between datasets of High-Learning and Low-Learning (as well as High-Exam vs. Low-Exam) are used to evaluate the status of research questions one and two.

Furthermore, the stationary probabilities of each state in the two high-achievement models (High-Learning, High-Exam) are compared to determine the evolution of interaction activity patterns in the high-achievement group. The same analysis is also conducted on the two models of the low-achievement group. Then, the interaction activity evolution of both two groups is detected, which answers research questions three and four.

Note

1 More details of HMMs could be found in the artilce from: https://www.quantstart.com/articles/hidden-markov-models-an-introduction/

References

Bahl, L., Brown, P. F., De Souza, P. V., & Mercer, R. L. (1986). Maximum mutual information estimation of hidden Markov model parameters for speech recognition. Proceedings of the *IEEE-IECEJ-AS International Conference on Acoustics, Speech, and Signal Processing, 1*, 49–52.

Baum, L. E., Petrie, T., Soules, G., & Weiss, N. (1970). A maximization technique occurring in the statistical analysis of probabilistic functions of Markov chains. *Annals of Mathematical Statistics, 41*(1), 164–171.

Ben-Yishai, A., & Burshtein, D. (2004). A discriminative training algorithm for hidden Markov models. *IEEE Transactions on Speech and Audio Processing 12*(3), 204–217. doi:10.1109/TSA.2003.822639

García, E., Romero, C., Ventura, S., & Calders, T. (2007). *Drawbacks and solutions of applying association rule mining in learning management systems.* Paper presented at the International Workshop on Applying Data Mining in e-Learning (ADML 2007), Crete, Greece.

Heckerman, D. (1998). A tutorial on learning with Bayesian networks. In M. Jordan (Ed.), *Proceedings of the NATO Advanced Study Institute on Learning in Graphical Models* (pp. 301–354). Springer Science+Business Media Dordrecht.

Jeong, H., Biswas, G., Johnson, J., & Howard, L. (2010). *Analysis of productive learning behaviors in a structured inquiry cycle using hidden Markov models.* Paper presented at the 3rd International Conference on Educational Data Mining, Pittsburgh, USA.

Jeong, H., Gupta, A., Roscoe, R., Wagster, J., Biswas, G., & Schwartz, D. (2008). *Using hidden Markov models to characterize student behaviors in learning-by-teaching environments.* Paper presented at the International Conference on Intelligent Tutoring Systems, Montreal, Canada.

Kwong, S., He, Q., & Man, K. F. (1996). Training approach for hidden Markov models. *Electronics Letters*, *32*(17), 1554–1555. doi:10.1049/el:19961080

Li, C., & Biswas, G. (2002). A Bayesian approach for structural learning with hidden Markov models. *Scientific Programming*, *10*(3), 201–219.

Martinez, R., Yacef, K., Kay, J., Kharrufa, A., & Al-Qaraghuli, A. (2011). *Analysing frequent sequential patterns of collaborative learning activity around an interactive tabletop*. Paper presented at the 4th International Conference on Educational Data Mining, Eindhoven, Netherlands.

Panuccio, A., Bicego, M., & Murino, V. (2002). *A hidden Markov model-based approach to sequential data Clustering*. Paper presented at the Joint IAPR International Workshops on Statistical Techniques in Pattern Recognition, Windsor, Ontario, Canada.

Rabiner, L. R. (1989). A tutorial on hidden Markov models and selected applications in speech recognition. *Proceedings of the IEEE*, *77*(2), 257–286.

Rabiner, L. R., & Juang, B. H. (1986). An introduction to hidden Markov models. *IEEE ASSP Magazine*, *3*(1), 4–16.

Romero, C., Romero, J. R., & Ventura, S. (2014). A survey on pre-processing educational data. In A. Peña-Ayala (Ed.), *Educational data mining* (pp. 29–64). Switzerland: Springer International Publishing.

Schwarz, G. (1978). Estimating the dimension of a model. *Annals of Statistics*, *6*(2), 461–464.

Soller, A., & Lesgold, A. (2007). Modeling the process of collaborative learning. In H. U. Hoppe, H. Ogata, & A. Soller (Eds.), *The role of technology in CSCL* (Vol. 9, pp. 63–86). Boston, MA: Springer.

7 Results and Discussion Based on the Case

Interpretations of HMMs Results

The first three models from datasets of High-Learning, Low-Learning, and High-Exam each have four states; the last model from the Low-Exam dataset has three states. We discuss the models in detail to demonstrate the HMM structure and BIC measures.

HMMs of High-Achievement Group in Learning Weeks

BIC measures in Table 7.1 indicate that the best number of hidden states in the High-achievement group in Learning weeks is 4; it is because when the number of hidden states is 4, HMM derived the smallest value of BIC (-128280).

Values of vector π in Table 7.2 show the chance that High-achievement learners engaged in each state in Learning weeks: 30.5% on State 1, 4% on State 2, 62.5% on State 3, and 3% on State 4.

Table 7.3 shows the transition probabilities among each activity state of High-achievement learners. The values in bold indicate the most likely transitions from a particular state to other states.

Based on the output probabilities in Table 7.4 (Please see the content in bold), frequent interaction activities in State 1 are Content, and Assignment & Quiz; the former took High-achievement learners 31.6% of engagement in State 1, the latter took them 48.7% of engagement in State 1; thus, we can define State 1 as Learning & Checking State. Similarly, State 2 is Forum (92.2%) State; State 3 is Performance statement (93.8%) State; State 4 is Group learning (99.1%) State. The values indicate the proportion of engagement that High-achievement learners spent on the activities in each certain State, which is the reason to define the State.

Figure 7.1 is a complete HMMs structure of High-achievement group based on Tables 7.2, 7.3, and 7.4 (only the values in bold are included in the figure). Figure 7.1 shows that: 1) High-achievement learners started from State 1 (Learning & Assignment State); there is a 59.6% probability for High-achievement learners to remain in State 1 to keep learning course content, and 40% probability to transition to State 3 to check their

Table 7.1 BIC measures of High-achievement group in Learning weeks

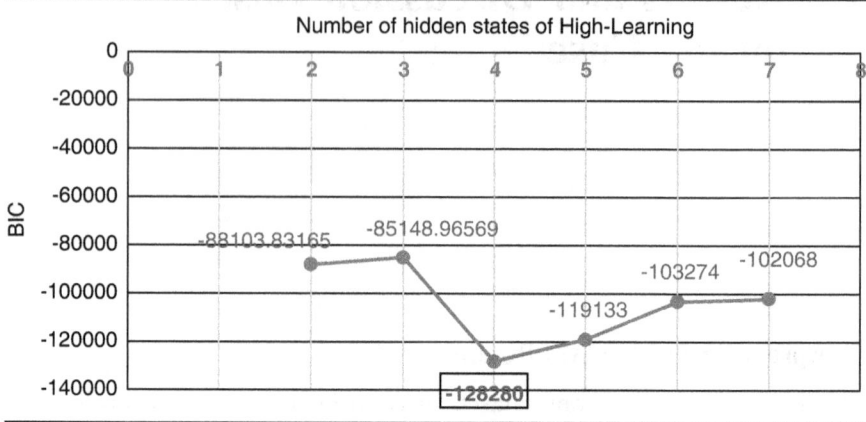

Table 7.2 HMMs initial probability vector (π) of High-Learning

	State 1	State 2	State 3	State 4
Π	**0.305**	**0.04**	**0.625**	**0.03**

Table 7.3 HMMs transition probability matrix (A) of High-Learning

A	State 1	State 2	State 3	State 4
State 1→	**0.594**	0.006	0.4	0
State 2→	**0.617**	0.003	0.312	0.068
State 3→	0	0.058	0	**0.942**
State 4→	0	**0.99**	0.01	0

Table 7.4 HMMs output probability matrix (B) of High-Learning

B	State 1 ↓	State 2 ↓	State 3↓	State 4 ↓
01 Introduction & Announcement	0.04	0.002	0.001	0.001
02 Content	**0.316**	0	0	0
03 Resource	0.058	0	0	0
04 Assignment & Quiz	**0.487**	0	0	0
05 Performance statement	0	0	**0.938**	0
06 Forum	0	**0.922**	0	0.008
07 Group learning	0.086	0.076	0.06	**0.991**
08 Course evaluation	0.013	0	0	0

Results and Discussion Based on the Case 69

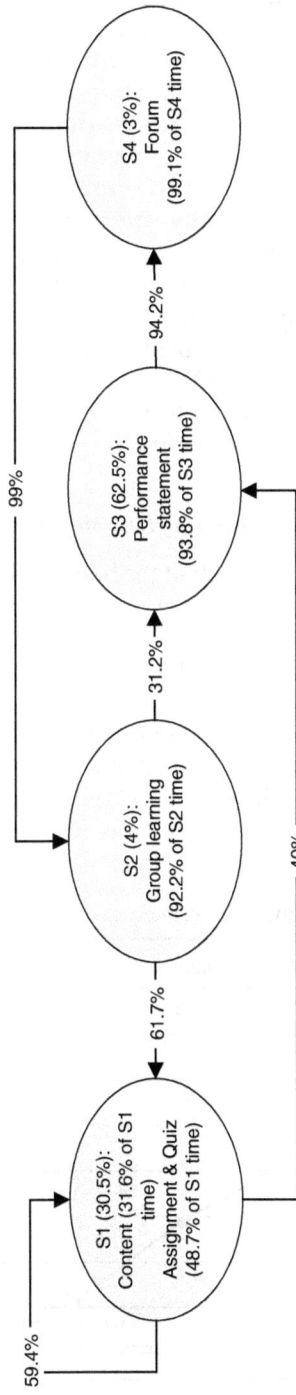

Figure 7.1 HMM of High-achievement group in Learning weeks.

performance statement. Furthermore, in State 1, learners engaged more in taking assignments and quizzes than in learning course content. 2) After learners transited to State 3 (Performance statement State), 93.8% of their engagement was in checking their own and their peers' performances. 3) Then, they transited to State 4 (Forum State) and almost totally engaged in the discussion. 4) After discussion, learners transited to S2 (Group learning state), and 92.2% of their engagement was in conducting group learning. 5) Then, they mainly transited back to S1 and S3.

Although there are four activity states in the model of the High-achievement group in Learning weeks, learners did not distribute their learning engagement evenly. They engaged most in S3 (62.5%) to check their performance statements, but only 30.5% in S1 to learn the content and assess their learning. Furthermore, they engaged less both in S3 (4%) to conduct group learning and in S4 (3%) to engage in discussions, even though group learning is one of the compulsory course plans, and discussions are always encouraged by the course instructor.

HMMs of Low-Achievement Group in Learning Weeks

BIC measures in Table 7.5 indicate that the best number of hidden states in the Low-achievement group in Learning weeks is 4 because HMM derived the smallest value of BIC (-33952.48376) when the number of hidden states is 4.

Values of vector π in Table 7.6 show the chance that Low-achievement learners engaged in each state in Learning weeks: 2% on State 1, 0.3% on State 2, 74.1% on State 3, and 23.6% on State 4.

Table 7.7 shows the transition probabilities among each activity state of Low-achievement learners. The values in bold indicate the most likely transitions from a particular state to other states.

Table 7.5 BIC measures of Low-achievement group in Learning weeks

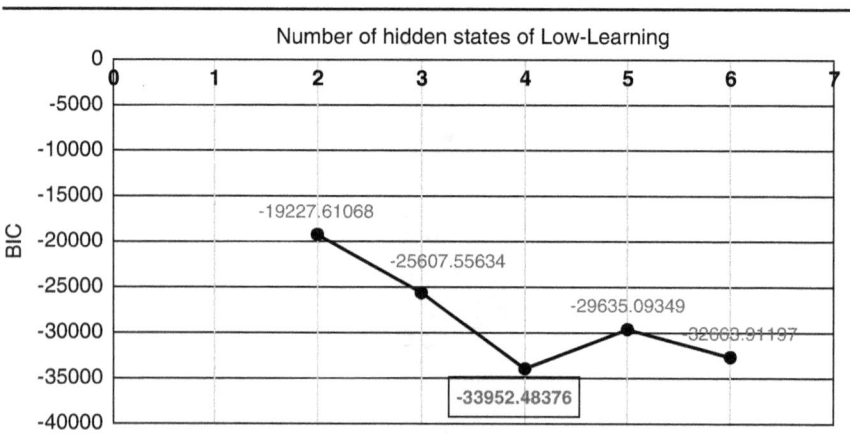

Table 7.6 HMMs initial probability vector (π) of Low-Learning

	State 1	State 2	State 3	State 4
Π	**0.02**	**0.003**	**0.741**	**0.236**

Table 7.7 HMMs transition probability matrix (A) of Low-Learning

A	State 1	State 2	State 3	State 4
State 1→	0.007	**0.993**	0	0
State 2→	0.009	0.293	0.016	**0.682**
State 3→	0	1	0	0
State 4→	0.059	0	**0.35**	**0.591**

Table 7.8 HMMs output probability matrix (B) of Low-Learning

B	State 1 ↓	State 2 ↓	State 3 ↓	State 4 ↓
01 Introduction & Announcement	0.007	0	0.002	0.024
02 Content	0.003	0	0.002	0.194
03 Resource	0.003	0	0.001	0.033
04 Assignment & Quiz	0	0	0	**0.332**
05 Performance statement	**0.63**	0	**0.994**	0
06 Forum	0	0.167	0	**0.361**
07 Group learning	**0.357**	**0.833**	0	0.049
08 Course evaluation	0	0	0	0.007

Based on the output probabilities in Table 7.8 (Please see the content in bold), frequent interaction activities in State 1 are Performance statement, and Forum; the former took Low-achievement learners 63% of engagement in State 1, the latter took them 35.7% of engagement in State 1; thus, State 1 is defined as Performance and Forum State. Similarly, State 2 is Forum (83.3%) State; State 3 is Performance statement (99.4%) State; State 4 is Assignment & Quiz (33.2%) and Forum (36.1%) State. The values indicate the proportion of engagement that Low-achievement learners spent on the activities in each certain State.

Figure 7.2 is a complete HMMs structure of Low-achievement group in Learning weeks based on Tables 7.6, 7.7, and 7.8 (only the values in bold are included in the figure). Figure 7.2 shows that: 1) Low-achievement learners started from State 1 (Performance and Forum State); there is a 99.3% probability for Low-achievement learners to transition to State 2 to discuss some topics in Forum. 2) In State 2, 83.3% of learners' engagement was in discussion. There is 29.3% probability for Low-achievement learners to remain in State 2 to keep their discussion, and 68.2% probability to transition

72 *Results and Discussion Based on the Case*

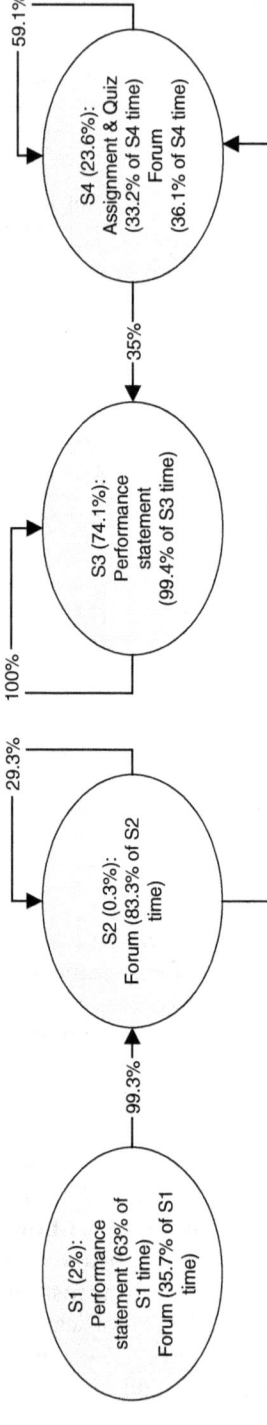

Figure 7.2 HMM of Low-achievement group in Learning weeks.

to State 4. 3) In State 4, 33.2% of learners' engagement was in conducting assignments and quiz, and 36.1% of learners' engagement was in the forum. Then, there is a 59.1% probability for Low-achievement learners to remain in State 4, and 35% probability to transition to State 3. 4) 99.4% of learners' engagement was in checking their own and peers' performance. There is a 100% probability for Low-achievement learners to remain in State 3.

Learners in Low-achievement group in Learning weeks did not distribute their learning engagement evenly. They engaged most in S3 (74.15%) to check their performance statements, but only 23.6% in S4 to do the assignments and quiz as well as participating in the forum. Furthermore, they engaged much less both in S1 (2%) to check performance and forum, and in S4 (0.3%) to engage in discussions. In the four states in the model, there is no evidence for these learners to learn and review the course content.

HMMs of High-achievement Group in Exam Weeks

When the number of hidden states is 4, HMM derived the smallest value of BIC (-69788), therefore, the best number of hidden states in the High-achievement group in Exam weeks is 4 (Please see BIC measures in Table 7.9).

Values of vector π in Table 7.10 show the chance that High-achievement learners engaged in each state in Exam weeks: 52,8% on State 1, 45.1% on State 2, 1% on State 3, and 1.1% on State 4.

Table 7.9 BIC measures of High-achievement group in Exam weeks

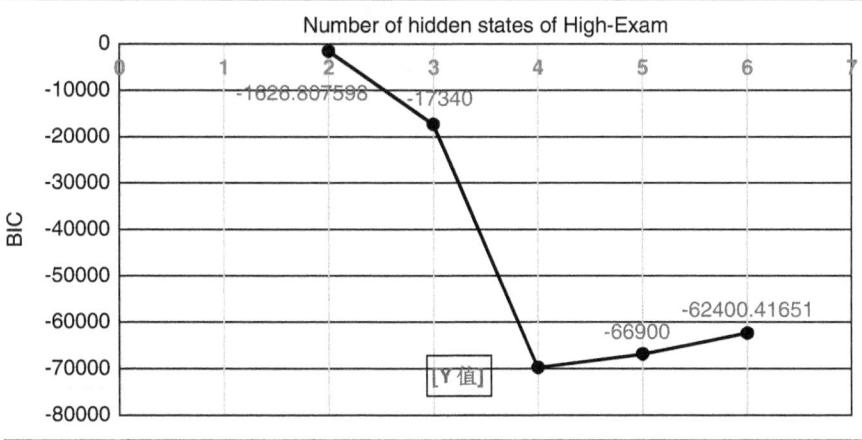

Table 7.10 HMMs initial probability vector (π) of High-Exam

	State 1	State 2	State 3	State 4
Π	**0.528**	**0.451**	0.01	0.011

Table 7.11 HMMs transition probability matrix (A) of High-Exam

A	State 1	State 2	State 3	State 4
State 1→	**0.636**	**0.364**	0	0
State 2→	0	0	0	1
State 3→	**0.822**	**0.178**	0	0
State 4→	0	0	1	0

Table 7.11 shows the transition probabilities among each activity state of High-achievement learners. The values in bold indicate the most likely transitions from a particular state to other states.

Based on the output probabilities in Table 7.12 (Please see the content in bold), frequent interaction activities in State 1 are Content, and Assignment & Quiz; the former took High-achievement learners 53.6% of engagement in State 1, the latter took them 35% of engagement in State 1; State 1 was defined as Learning & Checking State. Similarly, State 2 is Performance statement (99%) State; State 3 is Group learning (99%) State; State 4 is Forum (99%) State. The values indicate the proportion of engagement that High-achievement learners spent on the activities in each certain State in Exam weeks.

Figure 7.3 is a complete HMMs structure of the High-achievement group in Exam weeks based on Table 7.10, 11, and 12 (only the values in bold are included in the figure). Figure 7.3 shows that: 1) High-achievement learners started from State 1 (Learning & Checking State.); there is a 63.6% probability for High-achievement learners to remain in State 1 to keep learning course content, and 36.4% probability to transition to State 3 to check their performance statement. Furthermore, in State 1, learners engaged more in learning course content than in taking assignments and quizzes. 2) After learners transited to State 2 (Performance statement State), 99% of their engagement was in checking their own and their peers' performances. 3) Then, they transited to State 4 (Forum State) and almost totally engaged in

Table 7.12 HMMs output probability matrix (B) of High-Exam

B	State 1 ↓	State 2 ↓	State 3↓	State 4 ↓
01 Introduction & Announcement	0.016	0.01	0.01	0
02 **Content**	**0.536**	0	0	0
03 Resource	0.088	0	0	0.01
04 **Assignment & Quiz**	**0.35**	0	0	0
05 **Performance statement**	0	**0.99**	0	0
06 **Forum**	0	0	**0.99**	0
07 **Group learning**	0.01	0	0	**0.99**
08 Course evaluation	0.016	0.01	0.01	0

Results and Discussion Based on the Case 75

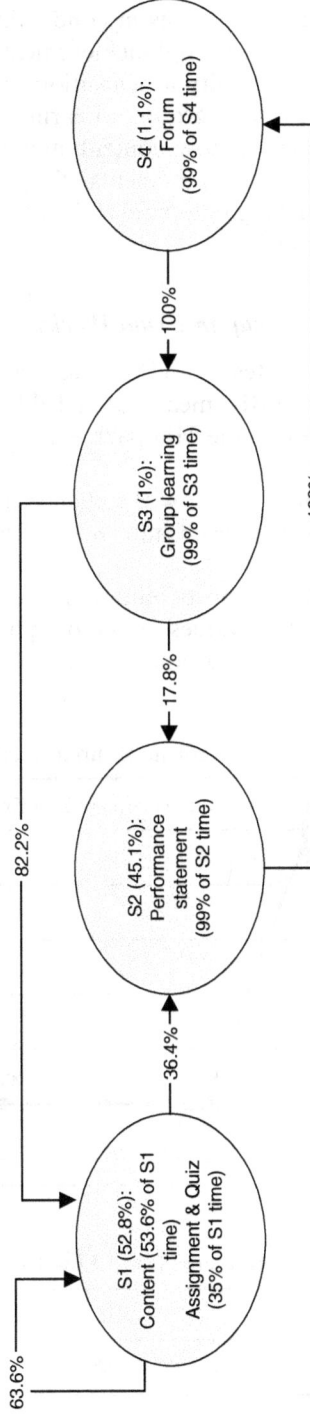

Figure 7.3 HMM of High-achievement group in Exam weeks.

76 Results and Discussion Based on the Case

the discussion. 4) After discussion, learners transited to S3 (Group learning State), and 99% of their engagement was in conducting group learning. 5) Then, there is 82.2% probability for High-achievement learners to transited back to State 1 and 17.7% probability to transition to State 2.

Learners in the High-achievement group in Learning weeks engaged most in S1 (52.8%) to review their course content and assignments, and S2 (45.1%) to check their performance statements. They engaged much less in S3 (1%) to conduct group learning and in S4 (1.1%) to engage in discussions when preparing the final exam.

HMMs of Low-Achievement Group in Exam Weeks

When the number of hidden states is 3, HMM derived the smallest value of BIC (-99999.09331) (Please see BIC measures in Table 7.13). Therefore, the best number of hidden states in the High-achievement group in Learning weeks is 4.

Values of vector π in Table 7.14 show the chance that Low-achievement learners in Exam weeks engaged in each state: 8% on State 1, 85% on State 2, 7% on State 3.

Table 7.15 shows the transition probabilities among each activity state of Low-achievement learners. The values in bold indicate the most likely transitions from a particular state to other states.

Table 7.13 BIC measures of Low-achievement group in Exam weeks

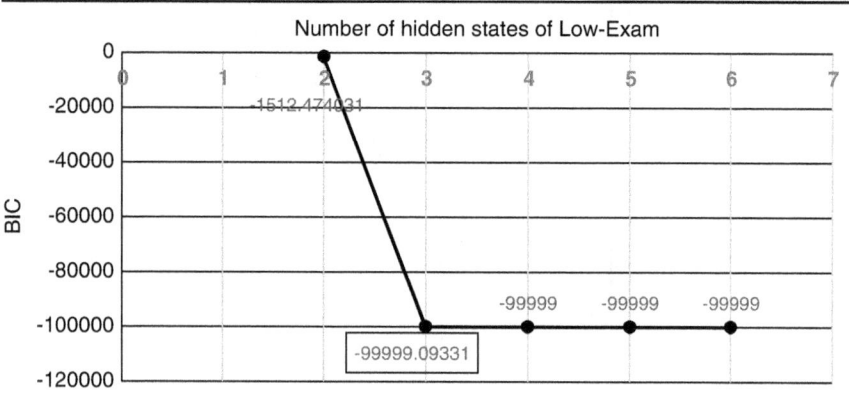

Table 7.14 HMMs initial probability vector (π) of Low-Exam

	State 1	State 2	State 3
Π	**0.08**	**0.85**	**0.07**

Table 7.15 HMMs transition probability matrix (A) of Low-Exam

A	State 1	State 2	State 3
State 1→	0.749	0.251	0
State 2→	0	0	1
State 3→	1	0	0

Table 7.16 HMMs output probability matrix (B) of Low-Exam

B	State 1 ↓	State 2 ↓	State 3 ↓
01 Introduction & Announcement	0	0	0
02 Content	0.083	0	0
03 Resource	**0.291**	0	0
04 Assignment & Quiz	0.083	0	0
05 Performance statement	0	1	0
06 Forum	**0.543**	0	0
07 Group learning	0	0	1
08 Course evaluation	0	0	0

Based on the output probabilities in Table 7.16 (Please see the content in bold), frequent interaction activities in State 1 are Resource and Group learning; the former took learners 29.1% of engagement in State 1, the latter took them 54.3% of engagement in State 1. State 2 is Performance statement (100%) State; State 3 is Forum (100%) State. The values indicate the proportion of engagement that Low-achievement learners spent on the activities in each certain State in Exam weeks.

Figure 7.4 is a complete HMMs structure of the Low-achievement group based on Table 7.14, 15, and 16 (only the values in bold are included in the figure). Figure 7.4 shows that: 1) Low-achievement learners started from State 1 (Resource and Group learning State.); there is a 74.9% probability for Low-achievement learners to remain in State 1, and 25.1% probability to transition to State 2 to check their performance statement. 2) After learners transited to State 2 (Performance statement State), 100% of their engagement was in

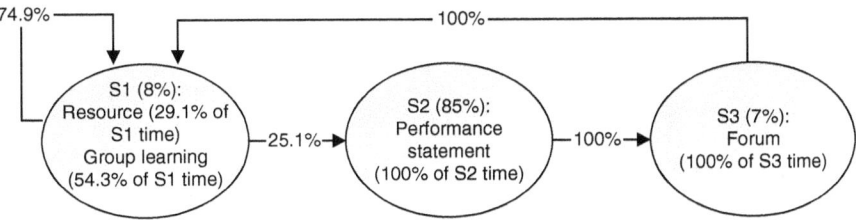

Figure 7.4 HMM of Low-achievement group in Exam weeks.

78   Results and Discussion Based on the Case

checking their own and their peers' performances. 3) Then, they transited to State 3 (Forum State) and totally engaged (100%) in the discussion. 4) After discussion, learners transited back to S1 (Group learning state).

Learners of the Low-achievement group in Exam weeks engaged most in S2 (85%) to check their performance statements, but only 8% in S1 and 7% in S3.

Generally, no matter what observable activities associated with each state or what transition probabilities between each state, the differences in activity patterns between two achievement groups in two course-processes are very clear. The differences of the High-achievement group between two course-processes are more in transition probabilities rather than observable activities associated with each state. But the patterns of Low-achievement group in two course-processes are very different in each activity state. The only engaging activity crossing the four patterns in two achievement groups and two course-processes is Performance statement, which is a very interesting phenomenon. The two activities mostly ignored by all the learners are Introduction & Announcement and Course evaluation.

The HMM approach offers a state-based analysis of learners' interaction activities; thus, the patterns of the two achievement groups in two course-processes are based on the different parameters in Figures 7.1, 7.2, 7.3, and 7.4, and these findings are interpreted to answer the four research questions proposed in this study.

Answers for the Research Questions

Research Question 1: High-Learning V.S. Low-Learning

The most obvious difference between activity patterns of two groups in Learning weeks is the observable frequent activities associated with each state, the distributions of engagement chance, and the transition characteristics (Please see Table 7.17, Figure 7.1, and 7.2).

High-achievement learners started their course learning from content and assignment & quiz, with an approximately 60% probability that they remained

Table 7.17 Distribution of major activities of two groups in Learning weeks

	State 1	State 2	State 3	State 4
Initial probability of each state	30.5%	4%	62.5%	3%
High-Learning	Content (31.6%) Assignment & Quiz (48.7%)	Group learning (92.2%)	Performance statement (93.8%)	Forum (99.1%)
Initial probability of each state	2%	0.3%	74.1%	23.6%
Low-Learning	Performance statement (63%) Forum (35.7%)	Forum (83.3%)	Performance statement (99.4%)	Assignment & Quiz (33.2%) Forum (36.1%)

in S1 to continue learning, a 40% probability that they transited to S3 to check performance statements and a 60% probability of learners engaged in Learning weeks during S3. On the other hand, High-achievement learners did not engage in group learning and forum discussions. By reviewing the forum records and group learning actions, we found that High-achievement learners only regarded Forum as a tool to conduct their group learning in the course context in which forum is a mandatory item in the course plan. This also explains why they almost exclusively transited from S4 (Forum state) to S2 (Group learning). After group learning,), High-achievement learners primarily (61.7% probability) transitioned back to S1 to focus on their own learning again, and they were also somewhat likely (31.2% probability) to transit to S3 to check their performance statements again.

However, Low-achievement learners conducted their learning in a very different way. Early in the course process, they started checking their performance statements (even there was no statement at the beginning of the course) and engaging in discussions in the forum. Then, they focused their attention on the Forum State. After that, with an approximate 70% probability, these learners transited to S4 to take assignments & quizzes (33.2%), and forum (36.1%), but with an approximate 30% probability they stayed at the forum. It can be found that, when remaining in S1 and S2, Low-achievement learners discussed the interesting Moodle function of learners' performance statements. After they finally transited to S4, they engaged in assignments & quizzes, and forum with a 23.6% probability. They mostly (59.1% probability) stayed in S4 to focus on learning, but they still transited (35% probability) to S3 to check the performance statements, and then they totally stayed there with 100% probability.

Reviewing the pattern of Low-achievement group in Learning weeks, it can be observed that, none of the first three states shows evidence of engagement with course content. Far from High-achievement learners, Low-achievement learners seemingly did not engage in the course content, which may be the primary reason why Low-achievement learners did not pass the final exam. This pattern of data also raises the questions of when and where did the low-achievement learners learn the course content? Given that learning the course content is the most important part of the course, it is striking that these low-achievement learners showed little engagement with learning in their data log activities. Furthermore, Low-achievement learners engaged in Assignment & Quiz and Forum, but these two activities are in S4, the last state in the pattern. It seems that Low-achievement learners were not active in the learning process.

The only similar state of the two achievement groups is S3 (i.e., Performance statement), but obviously, Low-achievement learners were more likely to check their own and their peers' performance than High-achievement learners. However, this activity was not helpful for them to pass the course exam. Based on the Initial probability of each state, Low-achievement learners put more than 74% of their engagement in S3 performance statement

(Please see Table 7.17) in Learning Weeks. This may be another reason why Low-achievement learners did not pass the final exam.

Therefore, generally, the interaction activity patterns of High-achievement learners group and Low-achievement learners group are very different in Learning weeks.

Research Question 2: High-Exam V.S. Low-Exam

The differences between activity patterns of two groups in Exam weeks are also obvious (Please see Table 7.18, Figure 7.3, and 7.4).

High-achievement learners engaged in Content and Assignment & Quiz with a 52.8% chance. With 63.6% probability, they stayed in this state to review their learning and transited to checking the performance statements with 36.4% of the probability. They only took around 2% of their engagement in Exam weeks on Group learning and Forum; we infer that the reason for the transition to S3 and S4 is to review their behaviors in these two states to prepare for the final exam. This also explains why after the review in S3 and S4, they mostly transited (82.2% of the probability) back to S1 to continue reviewing the course. Also, they were still interested in performance statements, so they transited to S2 with 17.8% of the probability.

Low-achievement learners engaged neither in Content nor in Assignment & Quiz, but in checking performance statements with 85% of their engagement in Exam weeks, which is NOT an item in the final exam. We found that they engaged in Forum to look for something related to the final exam with only a 7% chance, but almost no useful responses. S1 consists of Group learning (54.3%) and Resource (29.1%), which is a confusing combination of data-log evidence to remind the reader where the data comes from in the process of preparing for the final exam. By checking the course design, we found the reason for Low-achievement learners started from reviewing the resource, which is because there are several simulated tests in Resource, and maybe they placed their hope of passing the final exam on these simulated tests. Even like this, they still engaged less in Resource (29.1% of S1 time), but more in

Table 7.18 Distribution of major activities of two groups in Exam weeks

	State 1	State 2	State 3	State 4
Initial probability of each state	52.8%	45.1%	1%	1.1%
High-Exam	Content (53.6%) Assignment & Quiz (35%)	Performance statement (99%)	Group learning (99%)	Forum (99%)
Initial probability of each state	8%	85%	7%	
Low-Exam	Group learning (54.3%) Resource (29.1%)	Performance statement (100%)	Forum (100%)	

Group learning (54.3% of S1 time), and started their review from Group learning. It is hard to give a reasonable interpretation of what these students were trying to accomplish with this approach.

By the comparison, we found that the pattern of High-achievement learners is effective, while the pattern of Low-achievement learners is hard to classify as a successful pattern, which implies Low-achievement learners appear more opportunistic and inactive when preparing for the final exam. For example, although there are several simulated tests in Resource, High-achievement learners did not focus on these tests, but still reviewed the course content and took assignments & quizzes; however, Low-achievement learners only focused on these tests instead of reviewing over the course content with more effort; unfortunately, they can hardly be expected to succeed in the course by performing like this.

Thus, the interaction activity patterns of the High-achievement learner group and Low-achievement learner group are not the same in Exam weeks.

Research Question 3: High-Learning V.S. High-Exam

There is no extreme difference between the two patterns of High-achievement group in Learning weeks and Exam weeks. The frequent activities associated with the states are almost the same, as well as the distribution of engagement chance in the two course-processes (Please see Table 7.19) and the transition probabilities from S1 to Performance statement Sate, Forum State, Group learning State, and back to S1 and Performance statement State (Please see Figure 7.1 and 7.3).

However, from the small differences of S1 between the High-Learning pattern and the High-Exam pattern, we can still find some meaningful information. In Learning weeks, High-achievement learners engaged more in Performance statement State than in S1. However, in Exam weeks, they engaged more in S1 than in Performance statement State. Moreover, in Learning weeks, learners focused more on Content than on Assignment & Quiz in S1;

Table 7.19 Distribution of major activities of High-achievement group in two course-processes

	State 1	State 2	State 3	State 4
Initial probability of each state	30.5%	4%	62.5%	3%
High-Learning	Content (31.6%) Assignment & Quiz (48.7%)	Group learning (92.2%)	Performance statement (93.8%)	Forum (99.1%)
Initial probability of each state	52.8%	45.1%	1%	1.1%
High-Exam	Content (53.6%) Assignment & Quiz (35%)	Performance statement (99%)	Group learning (99%)	Forum (99%)

while in Exam weeks, they reviewed Content more than Assignment & Quiz in S1. These two differences indicate that, in the learning process, High-achievement learners preferred to take Assignment & Quiz to consolidate their learning and build knowledge construction. But in the exam process, the course content is their first choice to prepare for the final exam because Assignment & Quiz can hardly cover all of the course content, and the final exam is based on the content instead of assignments & quizzes. We infer that this is an effective strategy to help them pass the final exam. The differences also indicate that, in order to succeed in the course, High-achievement learners consciously adjusted their engagement in terms of different course processes, and conducted the course work with more intentional efforts instead of guessing the content of the final exam.

Basically, the interaction activity pattern of the High-achievement learners group is consistent from Learning weeks to Exam weeks), and learners consciously adjust their engagement depending on different course processes.

Research Question 4: Low-Learning V.S. Low-Exam

Not only there are differences between the pattern of Low-achievement group and the pattern of High-achievement group in two course-processes, but also the patterns of Low-achievement group themselves in two course-processes (Please see Table 7.20, Figure 7.2, and 7.4).

For the Low-achievement learners, the only focus remained the same in two processes is the engagement in checking performance statements. However, it is difficult to have a reasonable interpretation of the patterns of Low-achievements in two course-processes. Fortunately, these patterns may be regarded as an early warning signal to remind related learners and instructors in this specific course.

Unlike the pattern for the high-achievement learners, the interaction activity pattern of the Low-achievement learner group is not consistent from

Table 7.20 Distribution of major activities of Low-achievement group in two course-processes

	State 1	State 2	State 3	State 4
Initial probability of each state	2%	0.3%	74.1%	23.6%
Low-Learning	Performance statement (63%) Forum (35.7%)	Forum (83.3%)	Performance statement (99.4%)	Assignment & Quiz (33.2%) Forum (36.1%)
Initial probability of each state	8%	85%	7%	
Low-Exam	Group learning (54.3%) Resource (29.1%)	Performance statement (100%)	Forum (100%)	

Learning weeks to Exam weeks, and based on the educational outcome for this group, neither of these two patterns in Learning weeks and Exam weeks is effective.

Discussions Based on Four Research Questions

In this study, we present an exploratory learning analytics methodology, HMMs, for identifying interaction activity patterns from learners' learning traces within MPOCs context. Results illustrate the effectiveness of this learning analytics methodology of mining big data in online learning for (1) identification of activity patterns employed differentially in two achievement groups as well as two course processes, and (2) analysis of activity states distinguished by the relationship to engagement or counter-engagement status of activities.

Key results point to the value of analysis based on achievement groups and on course processes. The activity patterns of High-achievement learners group and Low-achievement learners group are different both in Learning weeks and in Exam weeks. The activity pattern of High-achievement learners group is more consistent from Learning weeks to Exam weeks, but learners consciously adjust their engagement depending on different course processes, which suggests the activity pattern of High-achievement learners evolves based on different course processes. The activity pattern of Low-achievement learner group is not consistent from Learning weeks to Exam weeks, and both of the two patterns in Learning weeks and Exam weeks are not effective, which means the activity pattern of Low-achievement learners may be inconsistent. These results support the belief that certain interaction patterns may distinguish the high-achievement learners from the low-achievement ones, and learners conduct their activity using different patterns in different course processes.

Also, through mining invisible states behind the observable activities by HMMs, results indicate that some important learning activities are related to either more or less successful performance in MPOCs context. In particular, engagement in Content and Assignment & Quiz distinguished High-achievement learners from Low-achievement learners, both during the Learning process and Exam process. Further, over-focusing on certain activities, such as Group learning, Forum discussion, and Performance statement, may provide warning signs of learners' low achievement in the final exam, which could be used to provide corrective feedback. In addition, High-achievement learners adjusted their learning strategies based on the goals of different course processes; low achievement learners were inactive in both learning and exam processes. For example, low achievement learners were used to disengaging from the course content, depending on other peers in learning, guessing issues in the exam, drawing exam clues from simulated tests and so on will NOT benefit Low-achievement learners in any course process.

In addition, a particular phenomenon crossing the four patterns generated by HMMs is that of engagement in Performance statement, which shows strong evidence that learners care about their own or peers' performance statements. Performance statements help learners to compare themselves with peers, and evaluate ranks in the whole learner group, which influences learners' engagement and efforts in learning. Therefore, the Performance statement function in LMSs can be a useful entrance to make some designs to highlight good performance, encourage inactive learners, provide effective suggestions, and improve learning. For example, instructors and designers can use data visualization to show the details of effective and ineffective performance and encourage learners to improve their engagement. Also, based on details of learners' performances, they can design direct links and entrances of specific learning resources in the Performance statement function to support learners showing low performance.

On the other side, another issue that is suggested by these findings is whether forum discussion and group learning are effective in MPOCs. Online discussion and group learning are prominent activities designed in many online courses (Chan, Hew, & Cheung, 2009; Gulbrandsen, Walsh, Fulton, Azulai, & Tong, 2015; Mason & Watts, 2012; O'Malley, 2012; Thomas, 2013). Advocates insist that online discussion can support active learning and knowledge building (Dillenbourg, 1999; Hew, 2015; Meyer, 2003). Similarly, many studies focusing on collaborative learning indicate that collaborative learning can facilitate learner higher-order thinking, and greater productivity; it can also help learners construct more supportive relationships to relieve isolation (Barkley, Cross, & Major, 2014; Gokhale, 1995; Mason & Watts, 2012; O'Malley, 2012). In contrast to the prior work of other researchers, the current finding suggests that learners engaged little in forum discussion and group learning, and these two activities seemed to have little effect on learners' achievement. These results do not necessarily suggest negative conclusions about online discussion and group learning in terms of the results of this study. However, I propose a different perspective on forum discussion and group learning in the MPOCs context, which reminds researchers to challenge stereotypes and review the influence of forum discussion and group learning on MPOCs learners with particular characteristics.

Focusing on the MPOC population is a salient difference between this study and previous research discussed in the literature review section. For example, Perera and colleagues focused on 43 learners in online collaborative learning (Perera et al., 2009). Similarly, Martinez and colleagues analyzed the action patterns of 18 elementary learners in collaborative learning (Martinez, Yacef, Kay, Kharrufa, & Al-Qaraghuli, 2011). Kinnebrew and colleagues compared the interaction behaviors of 40 8th-grade learners (Kinnebrew, Loretz, & Biswas, 2013). These studies focused on a small number of learners in a traditional school context and employed sequential mining techniques to investigate interaction actions, which are very different from our study identifying activity patterns in MPOCs population through HMMs techniques.

Although Jeong and colleagues also employed HMMs to investigate interaction patterns, the basic unit in the analysis was neither interaction activity nor interaction action; it was "activity-action". In addition, they especially designed a circle including five modules to represent the learning process, thus, the final patterns in both performance groups are linear ones (Jeong, Biswas, Johnson, & Howard, 2010). However, this study particularly identified interaction patterns on activity level, and the course was not particularly designed for any experiment. Thus, these results are close to the MPOCs situation in the real world, which can benefit more efficient learners and instructors on a larger scale.

References

Barkley, E. F., Cross, K. P., & Major, C. H. (2014). *Collaborative learning techniques: A handbook for college faculty*. San Francisco, CA: John Wiley & Sons.

Chan, J., Hew, K. F., & Cheung, W. S. (2009). Asynchronous online discussion thread development: Examining growth patterns and peer-facilitation techniques. *Journal of Computer Assisted Learning, 25*(5), 438–452.

Dillenbourg, P. (1999). What do you mean by collaborative learning? In P. Dillenbourg (Ed.), *Collaborative learning: Cognitive and computational approaches* (pp. 1–19). Amsterdam: Elsevier Science.

Gokhale, A. A. (1995). Collaborative learning and critical thinking. *Journal of Technology Education, 7*, 22–30.

Gulbrandsen, C., Walsh, C. A., Fulton, A. E., Azulai, A., & Tong, H. (2015). Evaluating asynchronous discussion as social constructivist pedagogy in an online undergraduate gerontological social work course. *International Journal of Learning, Teaching and Educational Research, 10*(4), 94–111.

Hew, K. F. (2015). Student perceptions of peer versus instructor facilitation of asynchronous online discussions: Further findings from three cases. *Instructional Science, 43*(1), 19–38.

Jeong, H., Biswas, G., Johnson, J., & Howard, L. (2010). *Analysis of productive learning behaviors in a structured inquiry cycle using hidden Markov models*. Paper presented at the 3rd International Conference on Educational Data Mining, Pittsburgh, USA.

Kinnebrew, J. S., Loretz, K. M., & Biswas, G. (2013). A contextualized, differential sequence mining method to derive students' learning behavior patterns. *JEDM-Journal of Educational Data Mining, 5*(1), 190–219.

Martinez, R., Yacef, K., Kay, J., Kharrufa, A., & Al-Qaraghuli, A. (2011). *Analysing frequent sequential patterns of collaborative learning activity around an interactive tabletop*. Paper presented at the 4th International Conference on Educational Data Mining, Eindhoven, Netherlands.

Mason, W., & Watts, D. J. (2012). Collaborative learning in networks. *Proceedings of the National Academy of Sciences, 109*(3), 764–769.

Meyer, K. A. (2003). Face-to-face versus threaded discussions: The role of time and higher-order thinking. *Journal of Asynchronous Learning Networks, 7*(3), 55–65.

O'Malley, C. (2012). *Computer supported collaborative learning* (Vol. 128). Berlin: Springer Science & Business Media.

Perera, D., Kay, J., Koprinska, I., Society, C., Yacef, K., & Zaïane, O. (2009). Clustering and sequential pattern mining of online collaborative learning data. *IEEE Transactions on Knowledge and Data Engineering, 21*(6), 759–772. doi: 10.1109/TKDE.2008.138

Thomas, J. (2013). Exploring the use of asynchronous online discussion in health care education: A literature review. *Computers & Education, 69*, 199–215.

8 Reflection and Consideration

Implications for MPOCs

The knowledge from this study can be used in several valuable ways.

First, this study offers a new methodology, learning analytics, for studying invisible patterns based on temporal and sequential characteristics of interaction activities in MPOCs settings from different achievement groups. This study showed that interaction patterns can be effectively identified by using HMMs at the activity level. This exploration confirmed the assertion that interaction patterns could be effective to identify strong learners and weak learners in MPOCs, which has been illustrated in other learning environments such as MOOCs, blended learning in higher education, and K-12 contexts. This finding is particularly important in MPOCs, because massive learners make it difficult for instructors to identify strong learners and weak learners depending on their daily online behaviors. Activity patterns enable us to give concrete examples of patterns associated with some effective and important learning activities in MPOCs, which helps instructors to capture and describe learners' performances.

Second, we can identify the most salient activity patterns in different achievement groups and present these to instructors, then design important activities with more facilitation such as Content, Assignment & Quiz, Performance statement, and Group learning. Previously, LMSs generally aim at supporting teachers and administrators, and they provide teachers with many features to create, manage and administrate online courses. These functions allow them to include different kinds of learning activities such as content, forums, quizzes, examples, and so on, and facilitate administrative issues such as enrollment, grading, and monitoring the learners' progress and performance. Therefore, LMSs typically do not focus on examining the individual differences and personal needs of learners, providing a little, or in most cases, no intelligent support or adaptive features for learners (Graf, Liu, & Kinshuk, 2010). By identifying the activity patterns based on the learners' traces in LMSs, more features and functions will be designed in LMSs, which can help instructors better understand the characteristics of learners' interaction, and conduct learner-centered online courses.

DOI: 10.4324/b23163-9

88 *Reflection and Consideration*

Thirdly, new efficient ways of using LMSs to achieve effective learning in MPOCs can be analyzed and evaluated, and then introduced to learners and instructors. Essentially, it enables LMSs to provide evidence-based feedback to learners during different course processes if their current behavior is more likely to be associated with positive or negative performance and identify problems. Therefore, this feedback may also help learners to rectify ineffective activity patterns and consolidate effective ones.

Further, the information provided by the current study contributes to valid learner learning models for adaptive learning on MPOCs and the future development of recommendation systems. Such as: identifying similar performances in terms of achievement, modeling learners' underlying interaction behaviors with LMSs denoting different patterns, analyzing the adequacy of different types of learners' learning models, and building recommendation systems based on different online learning groups in MPOCs. In this sense, it is necessary to conduct more investigation as to how LMSs can be adapted to specific learners. For that purpose, however, we have to gain more knowledge.

Reflections of the Paradigm Shift of the Research Method

Beyond the discussion of the study findings related to the four research questions, this study also encourages researches, educators, and administrators to reflect on the paradigm shift from variable-based research to event-based research in MPOCs and other settings. As mentioned in Chapter 2, the variable-based research paradigm focuses on the analysis of variance between independent and dependent variable(s); while the event-based research paradigm attends to interaction events and analyzes the (dynamic) relations between them.

The foundation of variable-based research is traditional statistical approaches. The logic of such kind of research is Null hypothesis significance testing (NHST), which emphasizes whether there is a significant effect or not between variables, and whether to support or discredit a priori speculations about some aspect of a population based on a small size of the sample (Gibson & Ifenthaler, 2017). Also, how much variance in a dependent variable can be attributed to one or multiple independent variables. The values of variables derive from scales, surveys, questionnaires, or by coding schema or counting procedures (Reimann, 2009). Because it is impossible to measure variables in real time through the entire learning process, the values of the variables can only be static outcomes at one or some particular time point(s). Most of the online interaction studies before 2010 are variable-based research; therefore, the limitation of these studies is inevitable, which could only investigate these static variables related to interaction, but not focus on the interaction itself.

However, learning is not only an outcome but also a process. In contemporary educational research, there is increasing attention, valuation, and inquiry devoted to the temporal and sequential character of interaction, providing important information in learning and instruction that will allow researchers to construct theories of how learners behave overtime at the micro-level. Therefore, it is important to realize that advanced temporal and sequential analysis of interaction events entails the shift from the variable-based research to the event-based research. By integrating the current findings with the opinions of Molenaar (2014), a number of challenges resulting from this paradigm shift are discussed here.

One challenge is how to define the unit of behavioral events in interaction research. Currently, there is no conceptual framework to articulate different levels of interaction units to frame sequential characteristics within related research questions. The information about the interaction behaviors commonly includes access time, time spent, textual data, learner ratings, and other details. In an event-based research paradigm, the unit of interaction behaviors cannot be limited to only one dimension. In my study, the fine-grained interaction behaviors online are defined by two dimensions: activity and action. An interaction activity is defined as a sequence of learner interaction behaviors within one LMS module with learning and instructional meanings such as forum, quiz, assignment, and so on. Interaction action is defined as the educationally meaningful typical behavior in an interaction activity such as view, delete, change, create, and so on. On the other hand, since human beings are subjects who perform interactions with other entities when decoding the secret of interaction, we cannot ignore the subjects conducting these behaviors, because our final purpose of decoding interaction is to investigate how humans learn and thereby improve human learning. Generally, the subjects can be classified by demographic or course information which has been generally used in previous variable-based research, such as learning contexts, tasks, achievements, genders, groups, and so on. In this study, I focus on the pattern of interaction activity based on different achievement groups in self-learning in MPOCs, which is a challenge to combine a specific interaction unit and a certain subject division. This kind of strategy could be used to combine different interaction units and different subjects. But, a conceptual framework articulating different levels of the unit of learner interaction is necessary, which can enhance conceptual clarity and provide ground for mining different patterns of interaction events in the real-time learning process.

A second challenge is how to divide time in the whole time span under investigation (Molenaar, 2014). Time is a complex construct in educational research. In previous research, researchers typically make artificial divisions of time, such as to divide the timeline based on key points (course beginning, mid-term exam, and final exam) in the course plan. Even now, in the event-based research emphasizing time and sequence, there is no framework accepted by most researchers to clarify the dimensions of time. The segmentation of time can be approached differently based on the level of instructional units, time units or units of time in which a construct is acting homogeneously (Molenaar, 2014). In this study, based on the course plan, the 20-week course is divided into Learning weeks and Exam weeks, which is not a very detailed division. This is because learning and exam are conducted with very different plans, and even within Learning weeks, interaction patterns may also differ within and across weeks which may impact differently on learners' behaviors. A goal of future research will be to identify and better describe the evolution of these patterns over time. Choices of 'cut-in-time' in the temporal analysis have important implications for the research and results (Molenaar, 2014); therefore, researchers need to explore and cumulate more practices to formulate clearer guidelines towards determining segmentations of time in the event-based research paradigm.

A third challenge is how to apply different methods to answer different questions (Molenaar, 2014). Although there are many emerging techniques in learning analytics and educational data mining, as was mentioned in Chapter 2, researchers are only at the beginning of the exploration of the effectiveness, stability, feasibility, and differences of these methods. Understanding the characteristics of these emerging techniques and frequently applying these methods in research practice can definitely enrich our understanding of which learning and instruction questions can be answered, and which method is most appropriate for specific kinds of research questions. For example, in my study, the findings suggest, for mining interaction patterns at the activity level in MPOCs, the temporal and sequential analysis based on HMMs used in the current study can be effective. If the purpose of the temporal and sequential analysis is to provide a description at the action level, then additional sequential mining techniques need to be employed to mine more details of learning interaction.

A fourth question is how to integrate or balance research that focuses on the micro-level and the theory resulting from the more traditional approach at the macro-level. Currently, the event-based research is data-driven, and the temporal and sequential information is captured by LMSs at the micro-level. However, most contemporary theories explaining the relation among different educational constructs are usually defined at the macro-level (Molenaar, 2014). This dilemma has been discussed in the literature review in Chapter 2. Most of the interaction research before 2010 is based on traditional theories and methods. Molenaar (2014) noted that the different levels of granularity between research unit and theory are a challenge for meaning-making, and researchers have realized the need for micro-level theories to support temporal and sequential analysis. Combinations of the event-based research and traditional variables can help make connections between the macro-level theory and the micro-level event. This study does some exploration into this combination of macro-level theory and micro-level events. First, it focuses on the temporal and sequential characteristics of interaction to idenfity which meaningful sequences of learning activities occur during learning and instruction. Second, it combines the activity patterns with the final course achievement to identify which patterns of interaction influence course achievement. This combination connects the results from the micro-level analysis with contemporary theories and approaches, and makes a meaningful explanation of the study in the context of the contemporary research literature.

A final challenge is how to develop new theories based on exploratory studies focusing on temporal and sequential characteristics of interaction events. A key limitation of employing contemporary theories to interpret the results from analysis focusing on temporal and sequential data is that these previous theories are neither derived from nor totally illustrated by these data. Thus, to some extent, simply linking these analyses to previous theories is challenging. Lending support from the theories and practices from the instructional design area may be a useful approach to develop new theories based on such exploratory studies. It means to effectively design instruction and learning at the micro-level first, then employ learning analytics approaches to investigate the behavior patterns in specific contexts. For example, first, to design subactivities in each module in LMS; then, to tag and track learning behaviors with temporal and sequential information; then, to mine the patterns through data mining techniques; finally, to analyze the results and make comparison with the contemporary theories to develop new ones. The whole process needs cooperation from different stakeholders such as instructors, course designers, learners, technology supporters, LMSs administrators, etc., which is complex and slow. The online course in this study can be characterized as having weak instructional design characteristics. For example, there are no fine-designed activities in the course content module, the only actions are to read the text and watch the videos. Without designing and conducting activities with specific educational meanings, it is hard to build useful theories based on the analysis of instruction and learning behaviors. The results of this study are only an initial attempt to describe and evaluate the efficacy of learning analytics in mining educational meaning from Big Data in education, which is far from developing new theories. More efforts are needed to construct studies that employ event-based methods in educational research and combine event-based methods with the variable-based approach. This may be a way to develop new theories, and connect them with the contemporary ones, which can ultimately enhance our understanding of learning and instruction.

Limitations and Future Plans

The current study makes the assumption that learners with different achievements conduct different interactivity patterns, and also learners conduct different patterns in different course processes.

Although the results of this study appear robust, these results are from comparisons of two (High/Low) achievement groups based on the grade C of the final exam, which results in a construct validity issue. Generally, there are grades of A, B, C, D, and F in a course. It is quite possible that the genuinely high achieving learners – those who earn an A or an A/B – conducted their interactions differently than a group of learners with a C. Therefore, in order to decode how learners conduct their interaction and learning, it is valuable to divide learners into more specific achievement groups and investigate more details of their interaction patterns.

In addition, the data were only from learners in one course, one semester, one major, and one open university, which is not sufficient to conclude that certain activity patterns or learning activities are definitely correlated with different achievements. This may not be true for other classes in the MPOCs context.

Since the data were only from learners in one class and one semester, the patterns could be substantially different in the case of other learners and other classes. For example, first-year learners, possibly because of their inexperience as MPOCs learners, may only engage more in the course content; while senior learners, because they have more experience learning in MPOCs, may be better able to manage their engagement, focus, and thus behave in different patterns. Furthermore, the results may vary based on learners' majors and courses they take. In this sense, the personal characteristics of the learners who choose a specific major or degree may influence the pattern of behavior in the LMS.

Therefore, one of the next steps is to apply this research line to more studies in MPOCs, which legitimizes the need for more focus on the background (learner and context) factors that could explain the differences discovered in different studies.

Moving forward, one research plan is to employ HMMs to investigate learners in different courses or majors, and then compare the activity patterns to identify the common and particular patterns across courses. The challenge is to explain why some interaction patterns are correlated with different achievements in different courses in MPOCs.

Another plan is to refine the classification of learners. This study only divided learners based on Grade C of the final exam, which does not precisely define the high achievement learner. Therefore, it could be more useful to divide learners into different achievement groups based on Grade A, B, C, and not pass, and then to mine the behavior patterns more precisely.

On the other hand, another issue concerns the model interpretation with more interaction details. Learners adaptively regulate their cognitive and metacognitive behaviors during learning is a premise towards achieving success with advanced learning technologies (Cerezo, Sánchez-Santillán, Paule-Ruiz, & Núñez, 2016). One of the future challenges is to design more effective learning strategies and then explain why some learners with different interaction patterns end up with different achievements in MPOCs. The attempt here is to develop new theories based on the combination of instructional design principles and learning analytics methods.

In this study, learners' interaction behaviors were defined in two levels: activity level and action level. The purpose of applying learning analytics methodology is to decode learners' learning at these two levels. Based on the previous discussion of this research paradigm shift, this inquiry will typically involve two steps. The first step is to assign specific labels to the HMM states by interpreting definitions, learners' engagement, and transitions by domain knowledge. The second is to investigate the interaction action details within each state to determine how and when learners interact with other entities at the action level. Therefore, in future work, it will be particularly interesting to employ additional learning analytics techniques to mine meaningful patterns of interaction action. Relating identified action patterns back to the specific context of learners' activity could help us to gain a better understanding of the relationship between learners' interactions and successful/unsuccessful learning in MPOCs.

This study did not aim to develop a general solution for the MPOCs context; rather, I tried to derive a large set of patterns that may suggest more specific, high-level interpretations of learner interaction to provide more efficient and effective understanding and to support recommendation systems and instructors' decisions in MPOCs. Also, with the exploration of future research, the experiences of event-based research will be greatly enriched, which will definitely contribute to the related research field.

References

Cerezo, R., Sánchez-Santillán, M., Paule-Ruiz, M. P., & Núñez, J. C. (2016). Students' LMS interaction patterns and their relationship with achievement: A case study in higher education. *Computers & Education, 96*, 42–54.

Gibson, D., & Ifenthaler, D. (2017). Preparing the next generation of education researchers for Big Data in higher education. In B. K. Daniel (Ed.), *Big data and learning analytics in higher education* (pp. 29–42). Switzerland: Springer International Publishing.

Graf, S., Liu, T.-C., & Kinshuk. (2010). Analysis of learners' navigational behaviour and their learning styles in an online course. *Journal of Computer Assisted Learning, 26*(2), 116–131. doi: 10.1111/j.1365-2729.2009.00336.x

Molenaar, I. (2014). Advances in temporal analysis in learning and instruction. *Frontline Learning Research, 2*(4), 15–24.

Reimann, P. (2009). Time is precious: Variable- and event-centred approaches to process analysis in CSCL research. *International Journal of Computer-Supported Collaborative Learning, 4*(3), 239–257. doi: 10.1007/s11412-009-9070-z

Index

Page numbers in **bold** indicate tables; page numbers in *italics* indicate figures

Abazi Bexheti, L. 38–9
achievement groups 7; high-achievement learners 2–3, 7, 62, **62**, 67–70; interaction patterns 7; low-achievement learners 2–3, 7, 62, **62**
advocates 1, 84
Allen, M. 17
Al-Qaraghuli, A. 37

Basis of Computer Applications 60
Baum-Welch (BW) method 63
Bayesian information criterion (BIC) 64; of high-achievement group in Exam weeks 73, **73**; of high-achievement group in Learning weeks 67, **68**; of low-achievement group in Exam weeks 76, **76**; of low-achievement group in Learning weeks 70, **70**
Betty's Brain 37
BIC. *See* Bayesian information criterion (BIC)
Big Data 2, 7, 91
Biswas, G. 36, 37–8, 54
brainwave data 33, 40
Broisin, J. 38
Brusilovsky, P. 38
BW. *See Baum-Welch* (BW) method

Chiu, C. 40
Chiu, M. 33
Choi, S. 18
Chu, K. C. 34
Chung, G. 24, 25, 26
collaborative learning process 35
computer supported collaborative learning (CSCL) 34

conditional probabilities 33
contextualized and differential sequence mining method 37–8
CSCL. *See* computer supported collaborative learning (CSCL)
Curran, V. 17

data. *See also* interaction data; collection 60–1; distilled for human judgment 32; pre-processing 61–2; transformation 62
data metrics in education 25
data mining method 34, 35
data-driven research 2, 59
Decision Trees 35
dependent variables 27
detection techniques 62
Digital Mysteries 37
Dillenbourg, P. 38
discourse, data 33
discovery with models 32
DMA. *See* dynamic multilevel analysis (DMA)
Doko, E. 38–9
dynamic multilevel analysis (DMA) 33
dynamic process dimension 25

EM. *See* expectation_maximization (EM)
enrollment, increase in 1
expectation_maximization (EM) 63

face-to-face interaction 6, 15
fine-grained sequential analysis 35
Finite State Machines 35
frequency analysis 33
Frequent Sequence Mining (FSM) 34

frequent sequential patterns 37
FSM. *See* Frequent Sequence Mining (FSM)
future plans 91–3

game-based learning environments 39
Generalized Sequential Pattern mining algorithm 36
Graf, S. 39
gStudy 35
Guerra, J. 38

Haenlein, M. 52
Hamiti, M. 38–9
Hidden Markov models (HMMs) 2, 35, 36–7, 63–5; of high-achievement group in Exam weeks **73**, 73–6, **74**, *75*; of high-achievement group in Learning weeks 67–70, **68**, *69*; initial probability vector (δ) of High-Learning 67, **68**; interpretations of results 67–83; of low-achievement group in Exam weeks **76**, 76–8, **77**, *77*; of low-achievement group in Learning weeks **70**, 70–3, **71**, *72*; output probability matrix (B) of High-Learning 67, **68**; procedures 64–5
high-achievement learners 2–3, 7, 62, **62**; BIC measures 67, **68**; HMMs of 67–70, **68**, *69*
HMMs. *See* Hidden Markov models (HMMs)
Ho, K. 17
Hou, H. T. 39
Howard, L. 36

Im, T. 17
independent variables 27
individual-level data 24, 25
initial probability vector 63; HMMs, High-Exam 73, **73**; HMMs, High-Learning 67, **68**; HMMs, Low-Exam 76, **76**; HMMs, Low-Learning 70, **71**
interaction, learner. *See* learner interaction
interaction action 10
interaction action level 60
interaction activity 10
interaction activity level 60
interaction data. *See also* data: individual-level 24; system-level 24, 25; transaction-level 24, 25; types, recorded by LMSs 24–6

interaction events, temporal and sequential characteristics 26–8
interaction patterns: achievement groups and 7; analyzing and detecting 7–8; definition 10–11; MPOCs 53–4
interaction research: with learning analytics 31–41; with log data 35–9; with log data in particular topics 39–40; traditional (*See* traditional interaction research)
Internet, distance education and 1. *See also* online learning

Jarvis-Selinger, S. 17
Jeong, H. 36
Johnson, J. 36
Jung, I. 18

Kang, M. 17
Kaplan, A. M. 52
Kay, J. 37
Kharrufa, A. 37
Khoo, L. 33
Kinnebrew, J. S. 37–8, 54
k-means clustering 36
Kumar, V. 25
Kuo, J. H. 34
Kuvalja, M. 27–8

lag sequential analysis 34
Lag Sequential Analysis (LSA) 34
Laplace approximation 64
learner interaction: activity pattern 63; importance of 5, 59; learner–content interaction 14, 16–17; learner–instructor interaction 14–15, 17; learner-interface interaction 15, 18; learner–learner interaction 15, 17–18; patterns 7; temporal and sequential characteristics 26–8; traditional interaction research, limitations of 5–6; traditional research on 16–18
learner–content interaction 14; traditional research 16–17
learner–instructor interaction 14–15; traditional research 17
learner–interface interaction 15; traditional research 18
learner–learner interaction 15; traditional research 17–18
learning: 'inherently sequential' process 10; interaction and 5, 6, 59

(*See also* learner interaction); traditional psychology and 26
learning analytics 10
learning analytics methodology 31–3; data distilled for human judgment 32; discovery with models 32; *versus* NHST method 31; prediction modeling 32; relationship mining 32; structure discovery 32
'learning by doing' 61
Learning Management Systems (LMSs): definition of 10; interaction activities in 25–6; Internet technology and 1; log data in 6–7, 10, 24–8, 35–9; MPOCs and 88 (*See also* Massive Private Online Courses (MPOCs)); trace data, analysing 54; types of interaction data recorded by 24–6
learning outcome metrics 25
Leem, J. 18
Lesgold, A. 35
Lim, C. 18
Lin, C. 40
Lin, Y.-R. 38
LIP-Miner algorithm 34
Liu, T.-C. 39
LMSs. *See* Learning Management Systems (LMSs)
log data, LMSs and: definition of 10; interaction research with 35–9; in particular topics, interaction research with 39–40; presenting interaction traces 24–8; utility of attaching importance to 6–7
log parsing 35
Logit 33
Loretz, K. M. 37–8, 54
low-achievement learners 2–3, 7, 62, **62**; HMMs of **70**, 70–3, **71**, *72*
LSA. *See* Lag Sequential Analysis (LSA)

Martinez, R. 37
Massive Open Online Courses (MOOCs) 2, 8, 9, 34, 52, 59; definition of 10; *versus* MPOCs 52–3
Massive Private Online Courses (MPOCs) 2; comparative research of interaction patterns 53–4; definition of 10; implications for 87–8; learner interaction research in 8–9; limitations and future plans 91–3; *versus* MOOCs 52–3
metrics in education: learning outcome 25; process 25

micro-level, interaction behaviors 6–7
micro-patterns (genomes) 38
Molenaar, I. 27–8, 89, 90
MOOCs. *See* Massive Open Online Courses (MOOCs)
Moodle 10, 25, 60; activity modules 61, 62
Moore's transactional distance theory 14–15
MPOCs. *See* Massive Private Online Courses (MPOCs)
Muhirwa, J.-M. 17, 18

Nesbit, J. 35
NHST. *See* null hypothesis significance testing (NHST)
null hypothesis significance testing (NHST) 8, 27, 31, 88

online learning: enrollment of, increase in 1; interactions in (*See* learner interaction); learner interaction in 5; learning analytics methodology 31–3; limitations and future plans 91–3; LMSs and (*See* Learning Management Systems (LMSs)); overview 1–2; research (*See* research)
outcome measures 24
output probability matrix: HMMs, High-Exam 74, **74**; HMMs, High-Learning 67, **68**; HMMs, Low-Exam 77, **77**; HMMs, Low-Learning 71, **71**

participants 60–1
Paulmani, G. 25
Perera, D. 35
Pinnell, C. 25
Plan Recognition 35
prediction modeling 32
pre-processing, data 61–2
Prevalla, B. 38–9
Problem Solving Genome 38
process measures 24–5
process metrics 25

qualitative content analysis 34
questions, research 59–60; discussions 83–5; High-Exam *versus* Low-Exam **80**, 80–1; High-Learning *versus* High-Exam **81**, 81–2; High-Learning *versus* Low-Learning **78**, 78–80; Low-Learning *versus* Low-Exam 82–3, **83**

real-time interaction behaviors 25
recommendation system 40
Reimann, P. 26, 27
relationship mining 32
research: data-driven 2, 59; design, MPOCs case 59–65; interaction (*See* interaction research); method, paradigm shift 88–91; questions 59–60, 78–83 (*See also* questions, research)
Rule Learners 35

Sahebi, S. 38
Sargeant, J. 17
'self-talk' 14
sequential analysis 33, 34, 39
Sharma, K. 38
SIS. *See* student information system (SIS)
Skog, T. K. 17
small private online courses (SPOCs) 8, 9, 52
Smyth, R. 18
Soller, A. 35
SPOCs. *See* small private online courses (SPOCs)
STAR Legacy Cycle 36
static outcome dimension 25
stationary probability 64, 65
statistical methods, traditional 7, 8, 27, 55
storing information 6; LMSs and 7 (*See also* Learning Management Systems (LMSs))
structure discovery 32
student information system (SIS) 24
summarization tables, data pre-processing and 62
Swan, K. 18
system-level data 24, 25

technology, learning methods and 1. *See also* online learning

temporal and sequential characteristics 26–8
Thurmond, V. A. 15, 16
TRAC 35
traditional interaction research: learner–content interaction 16–17; learner–instructor interaction 17; learner–interface interaction 18; learner–learner interaction 17–18; limitations of 5–6 (*See also* learner interaction)
traditional statistical methods 7, 8, 27, 55
transactional distance theory 14–15
transaction-level data 24, 25
transforming techniques 62
transition probabilities 64, 65
transition probability matrix 63, 70, **71**, 76, **77**

variable-based approach 27
Venant, R. 38
Verma, M. 27–8
Vidal, P. 38
video data 33
video learning data history 38–9
Viterbi algorithm 64

Wambach, K. 16
Wang, C. S. 34
Whitebread, D. 27–8
Winne, P. 35

Xing, W. 34
Xu, Y. 35

Yacef, K. 37

Zhang, D. 16
Zheng, J. 34
Zhou, M. 35
Zhu, G. 34
Zimmerman, T. D. 16–17

For Product Safety Concerns and Information please contact our EU representative GPSR@taylorandfrancis.com
Taylor & Francis Verlag GmbH, Kaufingerstraße 24, 80331 München, Germany

www.ingramcontent.com/pod-product-compliance
Lightning Source LLC
Chambersburg PA
CBHW050843160426
43192CB00011B/2133